THE TUTOR
THE SOLDIERS

GERMAN LITERARY CLASSICS
IN TRANSLATION
General Editor: KENNETH J. NORTHCOTT

Georg Büchner
LEONCE AND LENA; LENZ; WOYZECK
Translated by Michael Hamburger

Friedrich Hölderlin and Eduard Mörike
SELECTED POEMS
Translated by Christopher Middleton

J. M. R. Lenz
THE TUTOR and THE SOLDIERS
Translated by William E. Yuill

Gotthold Ephraim Lessing
MINNA VON BARNHELM
Translated by Kenneth J. Northcott

Friedrich von Schiller
WILHELM TELL
Translated by William F. Mainland

J. M. R. Lenz

THE TUTOR
—
THE SOLDIERS

Translated
and with an
Introduction
by
WILLIAM E.
YUILL

The University of Chicago Press
Chicago and London

The University of Chicago Press, Chicago 60637
The University of Chicago Press, Ltd., London

© 1972 by The University of Chicago
All rights reserved, including amateur and professional
performance rights. Published 1972
Printed in the United States of America

International Standard Book Number: 0–226–47210–8 (clothbound)
Library of Congress Catalog Card Number: 72–80812

CONTENTS

INTRODUCTION

Slightly but compactly built, a small head but most comely, its delicate shape matched by neat, if rather blunt features; blue eyes, fair hair; in short, a dapper little fellow, such as I have from time to time encountered among young men of Nordic races; a gliding walk, gingerly, so to speak, a pleasant but not altogether fluent manner of speaking and a general demeanour which, hovering between reserve and downright shyness, most fittingly became a young man.

Thus Goethe described the appearance of Jakob Michael Reinhold Lenz, who arrived in Strasbourg towards the end of April 1771 as traveling companion to two aristocratic officers from his Baltic homeland. Lenz's character Goethe summed up in the English word "whimsical," a term which hints possibly at an emotional instability that was ultimately to develop into mental illness. In Strasbourg Lenz found stimulating and congenial company, and it was here that he experienced the heyday of a tragically brief creative career. Although at that time, as now, the city was within the frontiers of France, it was a center of German intellectual life, just then beginning to stir with the ferment of ideas often known as the "Storm and Stress" (*Sturm und Drang*). It was in Strasbourg that Goethe had come under the influence of another visitor from the Baltic regions, Johann Gottfried Herder, who fired his interest in the national past and filled him with enthusiasm for Shakespeare and for folk poetry. With its emphasis on "nature" and on spontaneous feeling and expression, Storm and Stress was a reaction against the rationalism of the European Enlightenment which had dominated literature and philosophical thinking in

Germany since the beginning of the century. The first manifesto of the new movement was the collection of essays published by Herder in 1773, *On the German Mind and German Art* (*Von deutscher Art und Kunst*), containing notably his own rhapsodies on Shakespeare and on the spirit of folk poetry, and Goethe's profound study of Strasbourg Cathedral as a typical product of the German genius. In the same year Goethe published his epoch-making drama *Goetz von Berlichingen*, which treats an episode from German history in the manner of Shakespeare.

The drama was a genre much favored by the young writers of the Storm and Stress, for it alone seemed to offer ample outlet for their driving energies and sense of conflict. Even ephemeral satires on literary foibles and personalities were cast spontaneously into the dramatic mold, the customary metaphors of polemical prose being simply translated into terms of action and character, as in Goethe's *Gods, Heroes, and Wieland* (*Götter, Helden, und Wieland*) a dramatic squib aimed at a representative poet of Enlightenment, or Lenz's farce, *Pandemonium Germanicum*. For many poets of the movement, and particularly for Goethe, the drama was also a means of self-expression, a way of bodying forth inner conflicts and putting emotional dilemmas into perspective: "If I were not writing dramas," Goethe remarked in a letter at this time, "I should be done for." In some of his minor plays, *Friends make the Philosopher* (*Die Freunde machen den Philosophen*), *The Bower* (*Die Laube*), and *Myrsa Polagi*, for instance, Lenz, too, puts his immediate emotional situation or his wishful thoughts into dramatic form. The spirit of rebellion that is characteristic of Storm and Stress was frequently personified in Titanic heroes, so-called *Kraftkerle*, swashbuckling or genuinely heroic individuals in conflict with their age. Lenz's plays, like those of his contemporaries, are full of explosive action, rich in technical innovation, boldly experimental in their "open" form. His major dramas differ, however, in some significant respects from those of other Storm and Stress dramatists. He shared to the full their admiration for Shakespeare—in fact, Goethe credited him with special insight into "the extravagances and excrescences of the Shakespearean genius"—but his plays are not really Shakespearean. Their themes are topical rather than historical or legendary, their idiom realistic rather than rhetorical; they are not lacking in poetic quality but it is an astringent poetry of common experience and exact observation rather than the poetry of soaring imagination and invention: Goethe remarked of Lenz in *Poetry and Truth* (*Dichtung und Wahrheit*), "The poetry he could infuse into the commonest theme often astonished me." In speaking of the poet's inspiration Lenz invokes the myth of Prometheus, so popular with the Storm and Stress poets, but the central figures of his plays are not themselves Promethean—they are not *Kraftkerle* but victims.

Above all, Lenz's major works—*The Tutor* (*Der Hofmeister, oder Vorteile der Privaterziehung*), *The New Menoza* (*Der neue Menoza*), and *The Soldiers* (*Die Soldaten*)—show a degree of objectivity and an insight into social problems that is scarcely matched among Storm and Stress dramatists. Beneath the turbulent action of these works we may detect the regeneration in a more ample and sophisticated form of the didactic purpose that shaped the drama of the Enlightenment. It was that literary apostle of the Enlightenment, Johann Christoph Gottsched, who first regulated the German theater and attempted to make of it an instrument for the improvement by example and rational precept of the moral tone of middle-class society. To this end Gottsched promoted in particular a satirical brand of comedy, in which socially reprehensible foibles such as excessive piety, hypocrisy, snobbery, or avarice, were personified in the central character and exposed to ridicule. Although Gottsched, with his dogmatic and overliteral interpretation of Aristotelian "rules" and his simplistic notion of "probability," became the butt of succeeding generations, he did much by his energy and organizing skill to raise the standards of the German stage and lay the foundations of its later triumphs. The deathblow to Gottsched's reputation was dealt by Gotthold Ephraim Lessing, who brought a keenly analytical mind to problems of dramatic theory and initiated the Classical repertoire with his *Minna von Barnhelm* (1767) and *Emilia Galotti* (1772). In *Minna von Barnhelm* Lessing handled a potentially tragic theme in a fashion that was humanely sympathetic and infinitely more subtle than the satirical caricatures of Gottschedian comedy. In *Emilia Galotti* he created, in a setting that was audaciously topical, a sense of tragic vulnerability which was lacking in the pseudo-classical tragedies that had hitherto held the stage. The excitement that Lessing's dramatic achievement caused among the young men of Lenz's generation is reflected in the enthusiasm of Fritz von Berg and Pätus for *Minna von Barnhelm* in act 2 of *The Tutor*.

Lessing's dramas conformed by and large to the Aristotelian conventions: they observed unity of time, place, and action and avoided crass contrasts of mood. His analytical mind sought to represent the underlying unity of life's manifestations rather than their rich diversity; he conceded for this purpose a degree of abstraction and artifice that seemed irksome to dramatists of the Storm and Stress, who liked to think of the theater as a *Raritätenkasten* or peepshow. Although Lessing's fundamental rationalism may have been uncongenial to the younger generation, he had many ideas they welcomed: the notion of a characteristic German tradition and popular taste in the drama, for instance, a partiality for Shakespeare as opposed to the French models favored by Gottsched, the topicality of his themes and settings. Lessing accepted Aristotelian "rules" as pragmatic aids to the dramatist and did not regard them as necessarily binding on the true poetic "genius," who was aesthetically autonomous, his own lawgiver. As a rationalist, however, he considered the power of logical analysis to be the highest function of the human mind, so that it was in the detection of cause and effect amid the flux of human experience and in the representation consequently of continuous processes rather than disconnected events that the genius excelled. "Genius is concerned solely with events that are logically related," wrote Lessing, "chains of cause and effect."

This was too sober a view for Lenz. For him genius was not characterized simply by matchless power of logical analysis but by its well-nigh sensual force of imagination: "We call those minds geniuses," he declared, "which instantly penetrate whatever they encounter with such insight that their perception of it possesses the same value, range, and clarity as if it had been acquired by actual observation or by all the seven senses in combination." Lenz proclaimed the principle of poetry to be "imitation of nature." This is a perfectly traditional phrase, used by Gottsched and countless predecessors; by "imitation," however, Lenz understands a process infinitely more dynamic, evocative, and creative than anything envisaged by Gottsched or his authorities. Lenz speaks of the poetic genius as "reflecting its object," but he obviously regards the poet as more than a mere mirror of reality: for Lenz he embodies in the most striking fashion an essential human urge to re-create a world in miniature from the elements of God's created world, a microcosm from the macrocosm, "to penetrate with our gaze into the innermost nature of every being, to grasp and assimilate in a single emotional impulse all the rapture that exists in nature." With these words Lenz attributes a truly Faustian ambition to the poet: it is not the poet's function to combine in his imagination what are commonly called "the beauties of nature"; he must adopt a "standpoint," and the world he creates is ineluctably determined by his standpoint. Lenz implies a distinction between such inspired subjectivity and the artificially mannered subjectivity of the French Classical dramatist, whose chief merit consists in the construction of a plot, an arbitrary combination of events conditioned by the dramatist's frame of mind, so that the end product, in so far as it has any validity at all, is "not a portrait of nature but a likeness of the author's soul."

Holding such views, Lenz was bound to reject traditional dramatic conventions as an inhibiting or distorting medium placed between the mind of the poet and the essential reality that he seeks to depict. Needless to say, he repudiated the "frightful and miserably celebrated Bull of the Three Unities." The paramount aim of the dramatist must be to hold the *interest* of the audience, and he must be judged by his success in doing this. Although clearly he will not lightly surrender the practical advantages which unity of time and place offer him in the creation of theatrical illusion, the dramatist may have to sacrifice these advantages in order to depict adequately certain characters and their fate. And, indeed, "if moderation, purpose, and proportion are not already to be found in the soul of the dramatist, then the three unities will not put them there." As far as unity of action is concerned, "the mighty impulse of a dramatic action is generated in the soul of the poet like a clap of thunder in the heavens, and who should decree the path it should pursue."

Lenz's thoughts on the drama do not have the systematic stability of Lessing's. They are cloudy, speculative, and visionary, but somehow they carry conviction as expressing a deep sense of the relation between real life and its semblance on the stage. Lenz realizes that the effect of a drama depends ultimately on the dramatist's power to discriminate between contingent and essential truths. Although his *Remarks concerning the Theater (Anmerkungen übers Theater)* are couched in the flamboyant, provocative, and deliberately disjointed language affected by writers of the Storm and Stress, this should not blind us to the practical implications of his theories, which link him in a rather surprising way with the didactic approach of the Enlightenment. Lenz is no less conscious of his theatrical mission than Gottsched and he conceives it in even more ambitious terms. He visualizes an audience much wider than the culturally ambitious middle class that Gottsched principally aimed at. "My theater," he wrote in 1775 to his friend, the poet Gotter, "is, as I say, in the open air and in the sight of the entire German nation, in which the commoners are as important to me as the nobility." In justifying to Sophie von La Roche the alleged crudity of his themes, he reminded her "that my audience is the whole nation, that I can no more exclude the groundlings than I can exclude persons of taste and education, and that the man in the street is not so well acquainted with the ugliness of his vicious impulses and must needs have pointed out to him whither these impulses lead." Talking of *The Soldiers* he went so far as to describe himself in a Shakespearean phrase as "the stinking breath of the people." Lenz's concern to improve the morals of his day is even more radical than Gottsched's. His constant endeavor is to identify the abuses of the society in which he lives, "to represent the social classes as they really are, not as they appear to persons of the more elevated sphere, and to open up to the more compassionate, sensitive, benevolent, and charitable hearts among the latter fresh prospects and channels for their divinely inspired charity." His aim is "to stem the decay of morals that is creeping down from the illustrious ranks of society to the lower classes, who have not the means of defense against it available to their betters." Altogether, Lenz shows an informed interest in the life of the poorer classes and a sympathy for their problems that are unusual in his age. His admiration for the cheerfulness, industry, and common sense of working people is a feature of the unfinished drama *The Little Men* (*Die Kleinen*).

Lenz's thinking on the problem of dramatic modes is determined by this concern with the society of his age and nation. The rigid distinction which Gottsched had attempted to draw between tragedy and comedy on the basis of theme and social setting had been blurred by the development of "middle" genres—the sentimental comedy on the one hand and the tragedy of common life on the other—so that the situation when Lenz wrote his *Remarks* was fluid. Lenz bases his distinction not so much on thematic categories or on the social class of the characters in the drama as on the "popular taste" of his potential audience.

And here I find that this taste, whether in the case of the tragedy or the historical drama, invariably bursts forth (whether our aestheticians like it or not): "What a fellow! What fellows they are, to be sure!" In the comedy it is different. In the most trivial, farcical, and unforeseen of incidents in everyday life people cock their heads to one side and guffaw: "What a comedy! It's a real comedy!" groan the old crones. The main sensation in comedy is the event; in tragedy it is the character who creates events.... In my view the main idea of a comedy would always be the *affair*, of a tragedy a *character*.... [In a comedy] the characters are there for the sake of the action ... in a tragedy the action is there for the sake of the character.... A comedy without characters fails to interest us, a tragedy without characters is a contradiction in terms.

This conclusion, incidentally, is diametrically opposed to that reached by Lessing on the same topic, and it runs counter to the practice of the Gottschedian satirical comedy, which invariably revolved round the central character.

Gottsched had regarded comedy—restricted by him to middle-class themes, settings, and characters—as a more directly effective instrument of moral improvement than tragedy, in that he believed it made easier the necessary identification of the audience with figures and settings on the stage. Lenz also saw it as more effective for the additional reason that it had a more popular appeal than tragedy, which required for its appreciation a discriminating taste. The broad and fundamental appeal of comedy furnishes, in fact, Lenz's definition of it: "I do not call 'comedy' a representation which simply evokes laughter, but a representation which is for everybody. Tragedy is for the more serious-minded part of the public, which is capable of discerning heroes of the past in their true light and appreciating their merit." The "comedies" of the Greeks, maintained Lenz, were intended thus for the masses, and the "distinction of laughter and tears was nothing but an invention of latter-day critics who failed to perceive why the coarser element of the population is more inclined to laughter than to tears. . . . Comedy is portraiture of human society, and if this wears a grave aspect, then the portrait cannot well turn out hilarious." German dramatists, according to Lenz, found themselves in a special position: they had a duty to write "comically and tragically at one and the same time, because the nation for whom they are writing, or for whom at least they ought to be writing, is such a jumble of culture and coarseness, civilization and barbarism." The writer of "comedies" in Lenz's sense is thus preparing the way for the future tragic dramatist: "In this way the comic poet creates an audience for the tragic poet."

These considerations help to explain the designation "comedy" that Lenz attached to both *The Tutor* and *The Soldiers*, a designation that might otherwise strike us as being more in keeping with the ironic "black" comedy of contemporary playwrights than with the general usage of the eighteenth century. Lenz seems nevertheless to have had doubts about the proper description of the works: the manuscript of *The Tutor* has the subtitle "Lust- und Trauerspiel," i.e. tragicomedy, and Lenz refers to it in his correspondence occasionally as a tragedy. His perplexity was shared by friends and critics, some of whom referred to the play as a tragedy, while others called it a comedy. Before the publication of *The Soldiers* Lenz asked his friend Zimmermann to "delete the baroque title 'comedy'" and substitute the neutral term "Schauspiel," which may be here Lenz's equivalent to the word "drama" used by the critic Sebastien Mercier. One reason for the suggested change seems to have been Lenz's fear that the public, accustomed to the satirical comedy, might construe the play as a *Ständesatire*, i.e. an attack on the profession of arms in general—an impression he would be anxious to avoid, both because of his situation as companion to the von Kleist brothers and because he seems to have had military ambitions himself.

In *The Tutor* Lenz combines comic and potentially tragic elements in a way that seems more significant than the crude contrasts of the baroque drama that Gottsched had condemned. The combination of quasi-tragic fate and comic circumstance or comic character with potentially tragic situation constitutes a new kind of tragicomedy and marks Lenz's work as unique in its time—and possibly even ahead of its time, if we consider the view of tragedy and comedy as complementary aspects of human experience to be peculiarly modern. Läuffer's bizarre action, a drastic accommodation to the Procrustean bed of society, implies, whether Lenz was aware of it or not, a much bleaker view of the hero's situation than the compromise of, say, Lessing's *Minna von Barnhelm*, in which potentially destructive emotions are neutralized by reason and rendered socially innocuous. In the case of the other characters in *The Tutor*, it is true, something of the same bland solution is achieved through the liberal flow of sentiment in the closing scenes.

Elements of social criticism in the German drama of the eighteenth century are by no means confined to the Gottschedian comedy of types. A somewhat obscure dramatist, Johann Christoph Krüger, for instance, caricatured savagely in plays called *The Candidates* (*Die Kandidaten*) and *The Country Clergy* (*Die Geistlichen auf dem Lande*) the corruption and dissolute living of contemporary clerics. Lessing's *Emilia Galotti*—and subsequently Schiller's *Plot and Passion*

(*Kabale und Liebe*)—are political tragedies that attack the absolutism of the time which could be so easily put to evil ends by self-seeking counselors. Dramatists of the Storm and Stress dealt on occasion with the everyday problems of the humbler class; Heinrich Leopold Wagner, for example, depicted in a play entitled *The Infanticide* (*Die Kindermörderin*) the harshness of the law toward the unmarried mother who, in despair, killed her own child—an important motif, of course, in Goethe's *Faust*. The criticism of society in Lenz's plays does not quite conform to any of these patterns: it is more complex and more constructive, and it seems to probe more deeply into the fabric of society. It is pitched at a level between the broader political implications of *Emilia Galotti* or *Plot and Passion* and the concern of Wagner, say, with particular injustices. Lenz's views are less wildly tendentious than Krüger's, and his picture of society is both more ample and more finely detailed than that of the Gottsched school. He has an acute awareness of the social tensions that arise from friction between the classes, from class prejudice and exploitation. In spite of deliberately bizarre features of plot and character, the problematic situations that Lenz depicts strike us as authentic. This is not surprising perhaps if we bear in mind that certainly *The Soldiers* and very probably *The Tutor* are based on incidents from the playwright's personal experience.

In the case of *The Tutor* this conjecture is based only on the assertion made by a fellow countryman of Lenz many years after the play's composition that the scandalous events in it had taken place in an aristocratic family of his acquaintance and that he personally had known the models for Pätus and Bollwerk. However that may be, there is plenty of evidence from other sources that the circumstances of Läuffer's unhappy lot were not grossly exaggerated. The wretched tutor's interviews with Major von Berg and his wife in the first act of the play are almost copybook illustrations of what the satirist G. W. Rabener wrote in 1752: "And in order that the private tutor may not earn his money in idleness many employers are so ingenious as to require of him all branches of learning and, over and above this, all kinds of menial services; they would be only too glad if he were tutor and wigmaker and majordomo and tally clerk at one and the same time." Forty years later that celebrated authority on social behavior, Adolf von Knigge, had occasion to deplore the degrading servitude suffered by domestic teachers. "It cuts me to the quick when I see the tutor in many a noble household sitting deferentially mute at table, not daring to join in the conversation or place himself on an equal footing with the rest of the company, when even the children in his charge are given precedence over him by parents, visitors, and servants, whereas in fact the tutor, if he properly fulfills the duties of his office, ought to be considered the most important benefactor of the family." Of his own brief experience as a tutor during his Königsberg years Lenz subsequently wrote: "As my conviction concerning—or my prejudice against—this profession became ever more acute, I withdrew once more into my penurious liberty and never again acted as a private tutor."

However strong his prejudice against the institution of private tutors, or however great his compassion for Läuffer, it is primarily the social situation as a whole that Lenz criticizes. He stresses the disadvantages to both parties arising from such an arrangement: neither party is blameless, for Läuffer is at fault for selling the birthright of his liberty at the price of a daily roast and a glass of punch every evening. In his discussion with Läuffer's father (act 2, scene 1) the Privy Councillor puts the case most emphatically. It is he who acts the part of the man of good sense, the *raisonneur* whom we so frequently find as a stock figure in the comedies of the Enlightenment. It is true that Lenz, mentioning the play in his *Letters on Werther* (*Briefe über die Moralität der Leiden des jungen Werthers*) denies him this function. "People have not realized," he wrote, "that I was merely trying to give a strictly limited picture of things as they are, and the philosophy of the Privy Councillor has its foundations simply in his individual personality." This denial must strike us as disingenuous, however, since it runs counter to the theme of the play and the tenor of its arguments. At the same time, *The Tutor* is obviously more than a dramatized tract on educational policy. The main action which illustrates the moral is complicated by an interlocking subsidiary plot involving Pätus and Rehaar's daughter. In spite of the basically realistic idiom of the play, Lenz in fact shows some disposition to what might be called overorchestration of themes. The Prodigal Son motif, for instance, duplicated in the reunion of Fritz von Berg and Pätus with their respective fathers, is also reflected upside down, as it were, in the improbable coincidence by which Gustchen's benefactress, the blind old beggarwoman, turns out to be the repudiated mother of the elder Pätus. This kind of anagnorisis belongs to a tradition in the comedy as well as the novel and may have been devised by Lenz as an astonishing turn of events likely to appeal to his "groundlings." At any rate it permits the playwright to conclude his composition on a harmonious chord rather than a single note. The last scene of all constitutes a family tableau such as was not uncommon in the sentimental comedies of the eighteenth century. It would probably be wrong to assume that the implausible ending, the sentimentality of the concluding scenes, or, for that matter, Läuffer's lustless idyll were conceived by Lenz in a spirit of irony or intended as pastiche—although this is almost inevitably how they strike a modern audience. The almost instantaneous emotional adjustment to drastically changed circumstances which we witness here was in fact enjoined both by the Christian stoicism of the Pietists and by the rational optimism of enlightened philosophers. It smacks more, indeed, of the Enlightenment than of Storm and Stress.

The purely comic effects intended by Lenz in *The Tutor*—as opposed to the tragicomic situation of Läuffer or those effects which appear comic only to a modern audience—stem largely from the characterization. In certain cases—notably Major von Berg and Wenzeslaus—Lenz departs from his fundamental realism and introduces some element of caricature, no doubt on the principle he states in discussing his comedy *The New Menoza*, namely "the re-inforcement or heightening of the everyday characters" so as to make them "interesting and intriguing." Major von Berg and the schoolmaster embody a notion of whimsicality that was then considered typically English and which may in fact owe something to Shakespeare, Fielding, and Sterne. The reviewer in the *Frankfurter Gelehrte Anzeigen* was probably not the only reader to compare the Major, with his incongruous mixture of violent misanthropy and maudlin sentiment, to Fielding's Squire Western. The degree of exaggeration that Lenz allows himself is carefully regulated and never descends into the grotesque. The overall impression of the characters in the play is plausible. Their speech is vivid, colorful, and skillfully modulated to sustain the characters as Lenz conceived them. He handles with equal consistency the Major's tirades, the cranky homilies of the schoolmaster, the energetic preaching of the Privy Councillor, the rumbustious slang of the students, the schoolgirlish effusions of Gustchen with her sudden descents into the idiom of the hobbledehoy, and the mincing speech of Rehaar. It is an impressive range of idioms. Lenz is capable of a restraint and an economy that is rare in the wordy and heavy-handed satirical comedy of the Gottsched school. A brilliant example of his power to suggest obliquely the essence of a situation and the reactions of his characters to it is contained in the scene between Läuffer and Gustchen (act 2, scene 5), in which their predicament—Gustchen's pregnancy—is not, in the nature of things, stated or discussed but looms behind the dejectedly laconic dialogue. The drastic pruning by which this effect is achieved is revealed by comparison of the manuscript and the printed text, a comparison which calls in question, incidentally, Lenz's claim that he never "refined his plays once he had written them."

The Soldiers is more compact than *The Tutor*, less richly marked with life's diversity and the fantasy of the playwright. It moves with terrifying directness and speed toward its catastrophe and is an almost uniformly somber work to which the term "comedy" can be applied only in Lenz's idiosyncratic usage. The tragicomic ambivalence of *The Tutor* is barely manifest here: the comic elements are largely disjoined from the main theme and the central characters, attached for the most part to the eccentric personalities of peripheral figures. The moral of the play is added as a caption in a singularly stilted and unsubtle final scene. Here again it

would probably be wrong to assume that the suggestion put
into the Colonel's mouth by the playwright was intended
ironically: Lenz was composing at this time a treatise on the
problem of military marriages embodying suggestions which
he hoped to have adopted by the rulers of German states. All
the same, when we observe the extent to which the incidents
of the drama are drawn from Lenz's experience in Strasbourg,
the Colonel's proposal acquires very much the appearance of
an afterthought. Lenz himself conceded that this final scene
could be omitted altogether, provided he was able to achieve
his aim by representations at court. The play has in fact a
significance broader than the particular incidents on which it
is based and infinitely deeper than the propagandistic purpose.

In a diary which he kept during his stay in Strasbourg with
the von Kleist brothers Lenz gives a thinly disguised account
of events and personalities that correspond closely to some of
those in the play. Goethe, for whose benefit Lenz seems to
have deciphered his diary, reported many years later in his
autobiography that he had urged Lenz to incorporate the
incidents into a novel, but adds the comment that Lenz's
unruly genius was incapable of submitting them to the
discipline of a literary work. It is not clear why Goethe chose
to ignore that this is precisely what the dramatist achieved in
The Soldiers. Marie Wesener has been convincingly identified
as Cleophe Fibich, daughter of a Strasbourg goldsmith; the
role of Desportes corresponds to that played in real life by
Friedrich Georg von Kleist, while the youngest of the von
Kleists, who visited his elder brothers in Strasbourg, seems to
have acted the part of Murray. Lenz, with his propensity for
entanglement in the emotional affairs of his friends, appears
to have fallen in love with Cleophe himself and—rather like
Stolzius with Murray—had to act as the reluctant and jealous
recipient of amorous confidences. Otherwise, it is the figure
and situation of the young Count that seem to reflect Lenz's
part in the affair: we have Lenz's word for it that the Countess
de la Roche has something of the character of Sophie von La
Roche, a well-known writer of the time, for whom he conceived a sentimental attachment, referring to her meta-
phorically as his "mother." Even the burlesque episode of

Rammler and Madame Bischof may have been suggested by a further complication of Lenz's emotional life in Strasbourg, a misunderstanding by which his landlady, Luise König, ascribed to herself an amorous interest which Lenz intended for a mutual acquaintance, Henriette Waldner von Freundstein. This episode plays a major part in Lenz's Wertherian novel, *The Hermit* (*Der Waldbruder*). The catastrophe of the play, it should be pointed out, is pure invention.

It is understandable, then, that Lenz sent the manuscript of *The Soldiers* to Herder with the comment "that it involved half of my existence." It is understandable, too, that he was nervous about the play's local references. In another letter to Herder he wrote, "It is in the strictest sense a true story, experienced and prophesied in the innermost recesses of my soul. But, as I hope, masked so that the original, who is no Herder, will never recognize himself in it." Nevertheless he reflects in a further letter on the chances of the play's influencing the outcome of the real situation: "The girl who constitutes the central figure of my *Soldiers* is living at the moment in the sweet expectation of seeing her betrothed, who is an officer, return faithfully to her. Whether he does so or deceives her is in the lap of the gods. If he does deceive her, then the *Soldiers* could not be published soon enough, in order to ruin the man, or possibly to whip him back to his obligation. If he does not deceive her, then the play might possibly wreck her entire happiness and her good name, although nothing but certain details of local color are borrowed from her and I made the whole thing up." He made last minute efforts to conceal his authorship, suggesting to the publisher that it should appear under the fictitious name "Steenkirk of Amsterdam," denying categorically in correspondence that he had written the play and trying to persuade another dramatist, Friedrich Maximilian Klinger, to accept responsibility for it.

In *The Soldiers*, even more than in *The Tutor*, Lenz demonstrates an impressive grasp of dramatic structure and economy. The action moves with cinematic swiftness but never loses its coherence. The audience is barely aware of an "exposition" but deduces an already developing situation from hints and associations thrown up naturally in the dialogue: never for a moment is the dramatic interest allowed to slacken. In the later stages of the play a remarkable fusion of outer form and inner content is achieved as the accelerating tempo of the psychological development is reflected in the flickering series of scenes leading up to the explosive climax of the poisoning. In contrast to these fleeting impressions, an effect of structural solidity is created in the earlier acts by the regular alternation of locality between Lille and Armentières and by a pattern of symmetrical scenes underlying the flux of events—act 1, scene 3, and act 2, scene 3, for instance, or act 1, scene 2, and act 3, scene 2. The comic scenes in which Rammler is baited by his fellow officers act as counterpoint and retarding force in the headlong rush of the tragic action. A most striking contrapuntal effect is achieved at a pivotal point in the drama, the third scene of the second act: Wesener's aged mother croaks her somber song and counts her stitches like some malignant Fate as Marie and Desportes flirt in the next room. A baleful shadow seems to fall across the young people's brittle relationship.

Professor Walter Höllerer has pointed out that the varieties of speech in *The Soldiers* embody currents of thought and feeling typical of the age: the language of sentimentality, for instance, false in the case of Desportes when he woos Marie, heartfelt in the pietistically colored homilies of the Countess de la Roche; the language of rationalism, spoken with conviction by Eisenhardt and Spannheim, caricatured in the metaphysical balderdash of Pirzel; the threadbare courtly phrases attempted by the shopkeeper Wesener in his conversation with Desportes, which contrast with the rude vigor of the family quarrels. Only Marie and Stolzius speak a language which is for the most part unaffected, and the more they are overtaken by their fate, the more they express themselves in accents of simple feeling and naked despair, an idiom that elevates them above the historical context and stresses their common humanity as guileless victims of social privilege. Vain and frivolous as she is, Marie can hardly fail to inspire a deep pang of sympathy. Her ruin is as much the consequence of her father's ambition and greed as of her own folly and inexperience. Stolzius moves us as a pathetically ineffectual individual driven by an unbearable sense of injustice and loss to commit the one drastic action of a blameless life.

The Soldiers did not enjoy the critical acclaim accorded to The Tutor, which was for a time actually attributed to Goethe. A version of The Tutor was staged in Hamburg and Berlin in 1778 by the well-known actor-manager Friedrich Ludwig Schröder, who found in Major von Berg the kind of ambivalent tragicomic character in which he specialized. The play was also performed eleven times in Mannheim between 1780 and 1791. There seems to be no record of The Soldiers being performed during Lenz's lifetime. A collected edition of his works was published by Ludwig Tieck in 1828, but the first dramatist to take serious note of Lenz's work was Georg Büchner, who modeled characters and motifs in his Woyzeck on The Soldiers. It was Büchner who unearthed the chronicle of Lenz's illness written by his host in the Black Forest, Pastor Oberlin of Waldbach. From Oberlin's notes Büchner fashioned his moving short story Lenz.[1] The first known performance of The Soldiers appears to have been that produced by Max Reinhardt during the First World War. An opera by Manfred Gurlitt based on the play (1931) does not seem to have achieved much success, but The Soldiers has recently been brought to the notice of an international public in another operatic version by Bernd Alois Zimmermann (1957), which utilizes Lenz's text verbatim. The Tutor, of course, had already achieved fame in our time through the radical adaptation by Bertolt Brecht, first performed in 1949.

Lenz's career, termed "meteoric" by Goethe, barely survived the era of Storm and Stress. His reputation faded rapidly with his decline into illness and penury; by the time of his obscure death in Moscow he was almost forgotten. By then his contemporaries had outgrown the turbulence of their Storm and Stress, and the German drama had developed away from the terse and energetic realism of the 1770s: it had become

1. See the translation by Michael Hamburger in the present series: Georg Büchner, Leonce and Lena; Lenz; Woyzeck.

idealistic, fraught with profundities, staid and stylized in its forms, richly poetic in its language. This tradition, initiated by Goethe's *Iphigenie* and *Tasso* and continued with the great historical and philosophical dramas of Schiller, was further elaborated by the Romantics and major dramatists of the nineteenth century like Grillparzer and Hebbel. The tradition to which Lenz's major plays belong, a tradition of socially significant themes, topical settings, realistic idiom and "open" dramatic form was thus submerged almost at the outset. It reemerged briefly with Georg Büchner, who, however, was scarcely noticed during his lifetime, and then came into its own in radical fashion with the Naturalist movement at the end of the nineteenth century. The dramatic tradition of the Storm and Stress was ultimately transmitted by Büchner and Frank Wedekind to Brecht, who adapted it to express his Marxist ideology.

It would be wrong to imagine that Lenz was in his own day the kind of social revolutionary that Bertolt Brecht was. His works can be represented as relevant to the class struggle only by major surgery such as Brecht performed on *The Tutor*. It is true that Lenz criticizes features of what would now be called the Establishment, but he thought in terms of individual initiatives and moral choices rather than in terms of economically determined historical forces. He was essentially a reformer whose social thinking was conditioned by the rationalism of the Enlightenment and the postulates of Christian ethics that he had assimilated in his home and as a student of theology. He described the catastrophes that can eventuate when individuals are trapped between the social classes, but his solution was not to break down the barriers between the classes. On the contrary, he believed that these barriers should be reinforced by reason and more effectively sealed. A modern audience may be inclined to interpret the exhortations of Countess de la Roche to Marie Wesener as a hypocritical defense of her class interests. Lenz certainly did not conceive them in this way, as is evident from his identification of the Countess with Sophie von La Roche, whom he so deeply admired. Opinion about educational reform in *The Tutor* is not divided on lines of class, for the protagonist of a more liberal and democratic policy is himself a nobleman. Läuffer comes to grief because he occupies an anomalous position between the classes: his education gives him access on ambiguous terms to social circles to which, by breeding, he can never fully belong. He contrives in the end to assimilate himself to the peasant class only through the sacrifice of an essential human function. A modern audience may see in Läuffer's fate an ironic comment on the situation of the intellectual in a class society. The fact that Lenz probably did not understand it in this way does not, of course, invalidate such an interpretation.

We may ask ourselves all the same whether these two dramas can seem relevant to a modern audience otherwise than in interpretations or adaptations which place them in a special historical perspective by emphasizing economic factors and a class struggle of which the playwright himself can scarcely have had an inkling. Certainly, works which communicate such a vivid, coherent, and objective picture of a particular society at a particular time could be said to have an intrinsic interest—even if they are not immediately relevant in the sense that the special problems and circumstances they deal with could no longer arise. But do they have an interest and a truth which is more than antiquarian? It would be unjust, in fact, to regard *The Tutor* and *The Soldiers* as merely period pieces: in both plays Lenz has reproduced states of mind and motives that demonstrate convincingly the frailty of human resolve and the power of passion to overthrow reason. The very fact that the reforms he proposes in the rational spirit of the Enlightenment seem totally inadequate to curb the human waywardness he describes is a tribute to the continuing relevance of his insight into the nature of men. What Lenz wrote of *The Soldiers* applies equally well to both plays: "It is true and will survive, although centuries may stride contemptuously over my poor skull."

CHRONOLOGY OF
JAKOB MICHAEL REINHOLD LENZ

1751. Born in Sesswegen in the Baltic province of Livonia, 23 January (12 January, "old style"), son of Protestant parson, David Lenz.

1759. Family moved to Dorpat (Tartu or Jurjew) in Estonia, where Lenz's father ultimately became church *General-superintendent*.

1768–71. Theological studies in Königsberg; first major poems: of religious and didactic kind.

1771. Traveled with Friedrich Georg and Ernst Nicolaus von Kleist via Berlin and Leipzig to Strasbourg.

1772. Spring—traveled with the younger von Kleist to Fort Louis. Visits to Sesenheim, home of Goethe's former love, Friederike Brion. September—journey to Landau, return to Strasbourg at end of the year.

1772–74. Active in the Literary and Philosophical Society of Strasbourg. Works: *The Tutor*; translations of comedies of Plautus; *The New Menoza*; *Remarks concerning the Theater*; *Opinions of a Layman* (*Meinungen eines Laien*) (on theological topics).

1774. Affair with Cleophe Fibich that forms the basis of *The Soldiers*. Became companion to the third and youngest of the von Kleists, Christoph Hieronymus Johann. Autumn— left the von Kleists and earned his living by tutoring.

1775. Love for Goethe's sister, Cornelia Schlosser. May/June —meeting with Goethe when latter came to Strasbourg on his Swiss journey: close friendship between the two. Works:

Pandemonium Germanicum; The Soldiers. Feud with C. M. Wieland. November—helped to found a "German Association" in Strasbourg.

1775–76. Love for Henriette Waldner von Freundstein. Works: *Friends make the Philosopher; The Englishman (Der Engländer); On Soldiers' Marriages (Über die Soldatenehen).*

1776. 4 April—arrived in Weimar to join Goethe; in June, retired to live a "hermit's" life in Berka. Works: *The Hermit; Tantalus.* September/October—companion to Goethe's friend, Frau von Stein, in Kochberg. 1 December —obliged to leave Weimar because of some unexplained "tomfoolery."

1776–77. With Goethe's brother-in-law Schlosser in Emmendingen, then with friends in Switzerland; first signs of mental illness.

1778. Acute mental disturbance, attempts at suicide. January/February—with Pastor Oberlin in Waldbach, Black Forest, then with Schlosser and in care at various places.

1779. Brought back to Riga by his youngest brother, Karl.

1780–81. Attempts to settle in Baltic provinces and in Saint Petersburg.

1781. Instructor for a time at a private academy in Moscow. Renewed illness and increasing mental confusion.

1792. 3–4 June, found dying in a Moscow street.

THE TUTOR
or
The Advantages of
Private Education

A Comedy

CAST
(in order of appearance)

LÄUFFER, a private tutor

HERR VON BERG, Privy Councillor

MAJOR VON BERG, his brother

THE MAJOR'S WIFE

FOOTMAN

COUNT VERMOUTH

LEOPOLD, the Major's son

GUSTCHEN, the Major's daughter

FRITZ VON BERG, the Privy Councillor's son

PASTOR LÄUFFER, the tutor's father

PÄTUS, a student

FRAU BLITZER, landlady of Pätus

BOLLWERK, a student

FRAU HAMSTER, a town councillor's wife

FRÄULEIN HAMSTER, her daughter

FRÄULEIN KNICKS

HERR VON SEIFFENBLASE

TUTOR to Seiffenblase

WENZESLAUS, a village schoolmaster

MARTHA, an old woman, mother of Pätus senior

SCHÖPSEN, village barber

REHAAR, music teacher

FRÄULEIN REHAAR, his daughter

LISE, village maiden

PÄTUS SENIOR

ACT ONE

SCENE ONE

Insterburg in Prussia.

LÄUFFER: My father says I'm not fit for an academic post. I believe the fault lies in his purse: he won't pay for it. I'm too young for a parson, too well set-up besides, and too much acquainted with the world, nor will the Privy Councillor have me in the secondary school. So be it! he's a pedant, and the Devil himself is not learned enough in his eyes. After all, in six months I should have relearned as much as I knew when I graduated from college and consequently I'd have been too learned by half for a schoolteacher, but the Councillor thinks he knows better. He never calls me anything but Monsieur Läuffer, and when we talk of Leipzig the only things he asks about are Händel's teagarden and Richter's coffeehouse: is he being ironical or—? I've heard him arguing seriously enough with the deputy headmaster; I suppose he doesn't take me seriously. But here he comes with the Major; I don't know why, but I can't abide the sight of him, the fellow has something in his countenance I cannot bear. (*Passes the* PRIVY COUNCILLOR *and the* MAJOR, *bowing and scraping over and over again.*)

SCENE TWO

PRIVY COUNCILLOR, MAJOR.

MAJOR: What d'you think of that, then? Wasn't that a pretty coxcomb?

COUNCILLOR: Pretty enough, too pretty altogether. But what's he supposed to teach your son?

MAJOR: I don't know, Berg, you always ask such odd questions.

COUNCILLOR: No, seriously! After all, you must have some purpose in mind if you take on a private tutor and open your purse so wide all at once that three hundred ducats tumble out. Tell me, what do you mean to accomplish with this money? What will you require of your tutor for it?

MAJOR: That he . . . whatever I . . . that he should instruct my son in all the sciences, civilities, polite manners . . . I can't think what you're after with your quizzing. It will turn out all right in the end. I'll tell him everything in due course.

COUNCILLOR: In other words, you'll act the tutor to your tutor. But do you realize what you are taking on yourself in this matter? Tell me now, what is your son to become?

MAJOR: What is he . . .? A soldier, the sort of fellow I was myself.

COUNCILLOR: Omit the last, my dear brother. Our children need not become what we were: times change, manners, circumstances, everything changes, and had you become nothing more than the living image of your grandsire . . .

MAJOR: What the deuce! If he gets to be a major and a decent fellow like me and serves his king as honestly as I have done!

COUNCILLOR: All very well, but in fifty years we may have another king and a different manner of serving him. But I see I cannot enter into these matters with you; I would have to digress too far and to no good purpose. You can see nothing but the dead-straight line your wife has chalked along your beak.

MAJOR: What d'ye mean by that, Berg? Do not meddle in my domestic affairs, I pray you, as I do not meddle in yours. But look! There's your precious lordling of a son rushing out of school with a couple of hooligans. What splendid schooling, Sir Philosopher! A fine specimen he'll turn out! Who in all the world would believe that street urchin there is the only son of His Excellency, Privy Councillor to His Majesty . . .

COUNCILLOR: Let him be. His boon companions will corrupt him less than an idle fellow in a braided coat abetted by a stuck-up mistress.

MAJOR: You are taking liberties . . . Farewell!

COUNCILLOR: I am sorry for you.

SCENE THREE

Boudoir of the MAJOR'S WIFE. *The* MAJOR'S WIFE *on a sofa.* LÄUFFER *sitting beside her in an obsequious attitude.* LEOPOLD *standing near them.*

MAJOR'S WIFE: I have spoken to your father about the three hundred ducats fixed salary and we have agreed on one hundred and fifty. In return, however, Herr—what's your name? Herr Läuffer, see that you keep yourself in clean clothing and bring no discredit on our house. I know you are a man of taste; I heard of you while you were still in Leipzig. You know that there is nothing in the world nowadays that people take more heed of than how a person behaves.

LÄUFFER: I hope your ladyship will be satisfied with me. At least while I was in Leipzig I never missed a single ball, and I'll swear I've had over fifty dancing masters in my time.

MAJOR'S WIFE: Indeed? Show me then. (LÄUFFER *stands up.*) No need to be timid, Herr, Herr . . . Läuffer! Don't be nervous! My son is skittish enough as it is; if he gets a bashful tutor it'll be the end of him. Try again and see if you can do me a bow from the minuet; just by way of a sample, so I can see. Good, good, it will pass! My son won't need a dancing master for the moment at least! Do me a *pas* also, if you please. That will do. It will serve, once you have been to one of our assemblées. Are you musical?

LÄUFFER: I play the violin—and the pianoforte, at a pinch.

MAJOR'S WIFE: All the better. When we go down to the country and the Milchzahn girls pay us a visit I always have to sing the melody when the children have a mind to dance, but now it will be all the better.

LÄUFFER: Your ladyship drives me to distraction: where could there be in the whole wide world a virtuoso who might hope to match your voice on his instrument?

MAJOR'S WIFE: Ha, ha, ha! You haven't heard me yet. Wait a moment, do you know this minuet? (*Sings.*)

LÄUFFER: Oh! Oh! Forgive my rapture, this ardor that transports me. (*Kisses her hand.*)

MAJOR'S WIFE: Don't forget I have a dreadful cold; I can't help croaking like an old crow today. *Vous parlez français, sans doute?*

LÄUFFER: *Un peu, madame.*

MAJOR'S WIFE: *Avez-vous déjà fait votre tour de France?*

LÄUFFER: *Non, madame . . . oui, madame.*

MAJOR'S WIFE: *Vous devez donc savoir, qu'en France on ne baise pas les mains, mon cher! . . .*

FOOTMAN (*enters*): Count Vermouth.

(COUNT VERMOUTH *enters. He bows several times without speaking, sits down on the sofa next to the* MAJOR'S WIFE. LÄUFFER *remains standing awkwardly.*)

COUNT: Have you seen the new dancing master who has just arrived from Dresden, my dear lady? He's a marchese from Florence, his name is . . . To be frank, in all my travels I have not come across more than a couple who were to be preferred to him.

MAJOR'S WIFE: Well, I confess! No more than a couple! Indeed, you make me curious sir; I know how delicate a taste Count Vermouth has.

LÄUFFER: Pintinello, isn't it? I saw him dance in the theater at Leipzig. Nothing out of the ordinary . . .

COUNT: He dances—*on ne peut pas mieux.* As I was saying, dear lady, I saw a certain Beluzzi in Saint Petersburg who was superior to him. But this fellow has a sprightliness in his feet, something so untrammeled, so divinely nonchalant in his stance, in his arms, in his evolutions . . .

LÄUFFER: He was hissed at Koch's theater when he last appeared.

MAJOR'S WIFE: Pray take note, my friend, domestics do not join in the conversation of their betters. Go to your room. Who asked your opinion?

(LÄUFFER *retreats a few paces.*)

COUNT: The tutor intended for the young gentleman, I presume?

MAJOR'S WIFE: He's fresh from college. Be off with you! You can hear, can't you, that you're being talked about? That makes it all the more improper for you to stand about. (LÄUFFER *makes a stiff bow and goes off.*) It's intolerable, but one simply cannot find a gentlemanly fellow for one's money. My husband wrote at least three times to one of the professors there, and this fellow, such as he is, is reckoned to be the most gentlemanly in the entire academy. You can tell as much by the tasteless trimmings on his coat. Imagine: two hundred ducats for the fare from Leipzig to Insterburg and an annual salary of five hundred, isn't it shocking?

COUNT: I believe his father is the parson here in the town . . .

MAJOR'S WIFE: I don't know—it may be so—I have not inquired . . . yes, indeed, I'm inclined to think so. His name is Läuffer too, in fact; if that is so, then I suppose the youth is presentable enough. For the father is a veritable bear, at least he's bawled me out of his church once and for all.

COUNT: Is he a Catholic?

MAJOR'S WIFE: No, of course not, there isn't a Catholic church in Insterburg, you know. He's a Lutheran—or Protestant, I mean; he's a Protestant.

COUNT: Pintinello's dancing . . . It's true my dancing has cost me thirty thousand gulden or so, but I'd give as much again, if only . . .

SCENE FOUR

LÄUFFER'*s room.* LÄUFFER, LEOPOLD, *the* MAJOR.
LÄUFFER *and* LEOPOLD *are sitting at a table with books in their hands when the* MAJOR *bursts in on them.*

MAJOR: That's the way, that's what I like to see, nice and busy—and if the scum won't mind his lessons, Herr Läuffer, then let him have the book about his ears and flatten him, or, better still, just let me know. I'll set you by the ears, you villain, you! Look he's screwing up his mug again. Are you so touchy when your father tells you something? Who else should tell you? I'll have you otherwise or thrash you till your guts crack, sly boots! And you, sir, be diligent with him, I enjoin you, and none of your holidays and high days and recreations, I'll not have it. Ods Bobs, no one ever caught the *malum hydropisiacum* from hard work—that's nothing but an excuse thought up by you learned gentry. —How now, can he do his *Cornelio*? Leo! For heaven's sake, I beg you, hold your head straight. Chin up, lad! (*Straightens him.*) Damn and blast it, get your head out of your shoulders or I'll smash your backbone for you!

LÄUFFER: Your pardon, Major, he can barely read his Latin.

MAJOR: What? So the rapscallion's forgotten it! The last tutor told me he was word-perfect in Latin, word-perfect . . . Has he sweated it out, then?—I'll see you—I'll not be answerable at God's judgment seat because I didn't put the screws on you and you ended up a gallows bird like that young Hufeise or your uncle's boy Friedrich—I'll thrash the life out of you rather than see you turn out such a runagate wastrel! (*Boxes the boy's ears.*) Standing there like a question mark again, eh? He won't take a telling. Get out of my sight! Begone! Do I have to make you stir your stumps? Begone, I say! (*Stamps his foot,* LEOPOLD *goes off; the* MAJOR *sits down on his chair. To* LÄUFFER.) Remain seated, Herr Läuffer; I wanted to have a few words with you in private, that's why I sent the young gentleman away. You may remain seated—but properly, properly! Hang it all, you'll wreck that chair of mine if you perch on one corner . . . That's what the chair's there for, for sitting on. A much traveled man like you, and you don't know that yet? Listen now: I regard you as a nice, good-looking young man who fears God and knows his place, otherwise I wouldn't dream of doing for you what I'm doing. One hundred and forty ducats a year I promised you: that makes three—wait a moment—three times one hundred and forty, what does that make?

LÄUFFER: Four hundred and twenty.

MAJOR: Sure? Is it so much? Well, for the sake of round

numbers let us say 400 talers in good Prussian coin, that's your salary. Look, that's more than the whole province yields.

LÄUFFER: But begging your most gracious pardon, sir, your worthy lady spoke of 150 ducats. That would make exactly 450 talers, and those are the conditions I entered into.

MAJOR: Tush, what do women know of such things? Four hundred talers, Monsieur; you cannot ask for more in all conscience. The last man had 250 and he was as happy as a king. 'Pon my soul, he was a scholar, and a courtier to boot, everyone gave him credit for that, and you've a mighty long way to go young man, before you match him. What I'm doing for you I do for the sake of your father—and for your own sake, too, if you behave nicely and do as you're told; and I'm in a position to put you on your feet when the time comes, you can be sure of that. Harkee! I have a daughter who's the living image of me; you won't find her equal for looks in the whole of Prussia—everyone gives her credit for that. The girl has a totally different mentality from my rogue of a son. She must be treated quite differently from him! She knows her Christianity upside down and inside out, but nevertheless you shall do some Christianity with her every morning because she'll be confirmed soon and I know what parsons are. An hour a day in the mornings, and you'll go to her room—decently dressed, you understand, for heaven forbid you should prove such a filthy pig as one fellow I had who was determined to come to table in his dressing gown. Can you draw?

LÄUFFER: A little, sir. I can show you some samples.

MAJOR (*inspects them*): Quite charming! Very fine. That's good: you shall also teach my daughter to draw. But listen to me, my worthy Herr Läuffer, for heaven's sake, do not be too strict with her: the girl has a totally different mentality from the lad, God knows, it's as if they weren't brother and sister. Day and night she's crouched over books and tragedies, and the moment anyone says a word to her —especially me, she can't bear it from me—her cheeks are red as fire and the tears run down them like pearls. I'll tell you this, though: the girl's my only consolation. My wife's the bane of my life. She wants to rule the roost, and she's got more wit and guile than I have. And the son, that's her favorite. She means to bring him up by her own method; handle him with care, the boy Absalom, and he'll turn out such a hangdog as will profit neither God nor man. That I won't have: the moment he offends or scamps his work or hasn't learned his rule, just let me know and there'll be the devil to pay. But be careful with my daughter; my wife will try to persuade you to be strict with her. She can't abide the girl, I know, but if I see the slightest sign . . . I'm master in this house, you must know, and anyone who makes free with my daughter . . . She's my only jewel, and if the king himself offered me his realm for her, I'd send him about his business. Every day she's in my prayers, morning, noon and night, and if God should grant me the blessing before I die to see her furnished with a general or minister of state—for no other shall she have as long as she lives—then I'd gladly die a good ten years before my time. Just bear that in mind. And anyone who makes free with my daughter or harms her in any way—a bullet through his head and no nonsense! Bear that in mind! (*Exit.*)

SCENE FIVE

FRITZ VON BERG, GUSTCHEN.

FRITZ: You won't keep your word, Gustchen: you won't write to me when you're in Heidelbrunn and then I'll grieve myself to death.

GUSTCHEN: Do you think your Juliet can be so fickle? Oh, no; I'm a woman, it's only men who can be so fickle.

FRITZ: No, Gustchen, it's only women. Oh yes, if they were all Juliets! I'll tell you what: when you write to me, call me your Romeo—just to please me. I'll be your Romeo in all things—especially when I am allowed to wear a sword! Oh, I can even stab myself, if it comes to that.

GUSTCHEN: Away with you! Indeed you will—like it says in Gellert: he looked upon the point and blade and then his hasty hand he stayed.

FRITZ: You'll see soon enough! (*Catches hold of her hand.*) Gustchen, Gustchen! If I should lose you, or if uncle were to give you to another . . . That godless Count Vermouth! I cannot speak the thought, Gustchen, but you may read it in my eye. He'll be our Count Paris.

GUSTCHEN: Fritzchen! Then I'll do as Juliet did.

FRITZ: What? How? That's just make-believe—there's no such potion that sends you to sleep.

GUSTCHEN: Yes, but there are potions that give eternal sleep.

FRITZ (*throws his arms round her neck*): Cruel girl!

GUSTCHEN: I hear my father in the passage—quick, let's go into the garden! No, he's gone. We are leaving straight away after coffee, and the moment the carriage is out of sight you'll forget me.

FRITZ: May God never remember me if I forget you. But beware of the Count: your mother thinks a lot of him, and you know she would be glad to see the last of you—and by the time I've finished school, and three years at the university—that's a long, long time.

GUSTCHEN: But Fritzchen! After all, I'm still a child, I haven't even been to confirmation yet, but tell me . . . Oh, who knows how long it will be before I can speak to you again! Wait a moment, come into the garden.

FRITZ: No, no, papa has just gone past. Look, hang it all, he's in the garden. What did you want to tell me?

GUSTCHEN: Nothing . . .

FRITZ: Dearest Gustchen . . .

GUSTCHEN: You shall . . . No, I mustn't ask it of you.

FRITZ: Ask my life, my last drop of blood.

GUSTCHEN: We meant to swear an oath, the two of us.

FRITZ: Come on, then! Fine! Let's kneel down here by the sofa; lift your finger so, and I'll raise mine. Well, tell me what to swear.

GUSTCHEN: That you will come back from the university in three years and make your Gustchen your wife, whatever your father may say.

FRITZ: And what will you swear in return, my angel . . . (*Kisses her.*)

GUSTCHEN: I'll swear that I will be no one else's wife as long as I live, but only yours even if the Emperor of Russia were to come along.

FRITZ: I swear by a hundred thousand oaths . . . (*The* PRIVY COUNCILLOR *enters; they both leap to their feet with loud cries.*)

SCENE SIX

PRIVY COUNCILLOR, FRITZ, GUSTCHEN.

COUNCILLOR: What's the matter with you, you foolish children? Why are you trembling? Come along, tell me everything. What have you been doing here? You were down on your knees, the two of you. Be so kind as to answer me, Master Fritz—this instant! What were you up to?

FRITZ: Me, dear papa?

COUNCILLOR: Me? And in such a tone of wonder? You see? I notice everything. You'd like to tell me a lie now, but either you're too stupid or too frightened to do it and you think you can get out of your fix with your "me?" . . . And you, niece? I know Gustchen won't keep anything hidden from me.

GUSTCHEN: (*falls at his feet*): Oh, father . . .

COUNCILLOR: (*lifts her up and kisses her*): Do you want me for a father? Too soon, my child, too soon, Gustchen, my child. You haven't even been confirmed yet. For why should I conceal that I overheard you both. That was a very silly prank on the part of both of you—especially you, you great big, sensible Master Fritz; you'll soon have a beard like me and don a wig and bear a sword. Fie, I thought I had a son with more sense. This sort of thing makes you a whole year younger and means you must stay on longer at school. And you, Gustchen, I must tell you, too, that it ill becomes you at your age to act so childishly. What sort of fables have you been playing at here? What manner of oaths have you sworn that you'll both of you break as sure as I'm talking to you now. Do you think you're of an age to swear such oaths, or do you think an oath is a children's game like hide-and-seek or blind-man's-buff? Learn to understand what an oath is: first learn to tremble at it—and only then dare to swear it. A perjurer, you must realize, is the most shameful and the most wretched creature under the sun. Such a man may look neither at the heaven he has denied nor at his fellow men, who shun him and who avoid his company more scrupulously than they would a snake or a dog of uncertain temper.

FRITZ: But I mean to keep my oath.

COUNCILLOR: Indeed, Romeo? Ha! You can even stab yourself, if it comes to that. You have sworn such oaths as make my hair stand on end. So you intend to keep your oath?

FRITZ: Yes, papa, by God! I mean to keep it.

COUNCILLOR: An oath to keep an oath! I'll let your headmaster know of this. He shall put you down a class for a couple of weeks, Master Fritz; do not be so free in future with your oaths. And on what do you swear? Does it stand in your power to perform what you promise? You want to marry Gustchen! But think! Do you know what sort of business marriage is! Go ahead and marry her, take her to college with you. No? I do not mind you enjoying each other's company, nor being fond of each other, nor telling each other how much you care; but you mustn't do anything foolish, do not ape your elders until you are as grown-up as we are. Do not seek to act the fables hatched in the unbridled fancy of a starveling poet that have no shadow of reality these days in our world. Go away, both of you! I shall tell no one of this so that you need not blush when you see me. But from now on you shall not see each other except when other people are present. Do you understand? Nor write to each other any letters but such as others may read—and once a month at that, at most once every three weeks; and the moment a secret note to Master Fritz or Miss Gustchen is discovered—then the young gentleman will find himself a soldier and the young lady in a nunnery

until they learn more sense. Do you understand that?
Now—take your leave of each other, here, in my presence.
The carriage is ready, the Major's dying to be off, my
sister-in-law has had her coffee. Say good-bye: you needn't
be shy in front of me. Quickly now, embrace each other!
(FRITZ *and* GUSTCHEN *embrace, trembling.*) And now,
Gustchen, my daughter, since you seem to like that word,
(*lifts her up and kisses her,*) a thousand times adieu, and be
respectful to your mother, whatever she may say to you.
Be off with you, now. (GUSTCHEN *takes a few steps, looks
round;* FRITZ *rushes weeping into her arms.*) These two
idiots will break my heart! If only the Major had more
sense, or his wife were less of a shrew!

ACT TWO

SCENE ONE

PASTOR LÄUFFER, PRIVY COUNCILLOR.

COUNCILLOR: I'm sorry for him—and even sorrier for you, pastor, that you have such a son.

PASTOR: I beg your pardon, Your Honor, but I cannot complain of my son: he's a virtuous and accomplished youth, everyone, including Your Honor's brother and sister-in-law, must admit that.

COUNCILLOR: I don't deny him that, but he's a fool and has only himself to thank for all his vexations. He ought to thank his lucky stars that my brother's beginning to rue the money he laid out for a private tutor.

PASTOR: But just think of it: no more than a hundred ducats, a hundred paltry ducats. After all, he promised him three hundred the first year, but in the end he paid him only one hundred and forty. Now, at the end of his second year, although my son's work is increasing all the time, he paid him one hundred, and at the beginning of the third year he thinks even that's too much. You'll pardon me, but that's quite improper!

COUNCILLOR: Have done with this, do! I could have told you people that beforehand; anyway, you ought to thank God if the Major were to take your son by the scruff of the neck and throw him out of the house. What's he doing there, tell me that, sir! Do you seek to be a father to your child and yet close your eyes, your mouth, and your ears to everything that affects his happiness? Idling his days away and expecting to be paid for it? Loafing away the noblest hours of the day with a young gentleman who has no wish to learn but whom he can't afford to offend, and pining away like a slave on a chain the remaining hours that should be devoted to the necessities of life, eating and sleeping; hanging on the whims of her ladyship and conning the crotchets of his lordship; eating when he's full and fasting when he's hungry, drinking punch when he wants to piss, playing cards when he's got the runs. Without freedom life goes downhill backwards; freedom is man's element as water to a fish, and a man who surrenders his freedom poisons the noblest spirits of his blood, nips in the bud the sweetest of life's pleasures, and does himself to death.

PASTOR: But—I beg your pardon—every private tutor has to put up with that, after all; one cannot always have one's own way, and my son could put up with that all right, only—

COUNCILLOR: So much the worse if he puts up with it; he has renounced the privileges of man, who must be free to live by his own principles, otherwise he's not a man. Let those wretches who are incapable of elevating their notions of happiness beyond eating and drinking, let them allow themselves to be fed to death in a cage; but an educated man, a man who feels the nobility of his own soul, who ought not to shun death so much as an act that runs counter to his principles . . .

PASTOR: But what can we do in this world of ours? Whatever would my son do if your brother were to give him notice?

COUNCILLOR: Let the fellow learn a trade, so that he can make himself useful to the state. Damn it all, pastor, you didn't bring him up to be a flunky, and what is he but a flunky if he sells his freedom to a private individual for a handful of ducats? He's nothing but a slave, and his master has un-limited power over him, but he's learned enough at college to forestall the impertinent impositions of his employers and thus to give a polish to his servility. That's what I call a fine gentleman, a peerless fellow—a peerless rogue, rather, who, instead of devoting his faculties and his wits to the general good, employs them to buttress the lunacies of a vapid madame and a half-baked officer that day by day eat deeper like a cancer and finally grow incurable. And what is the gain in the long run? A roast at every lunch and every evening a glass of punch—and a good helping of bile that rises in his gorge by day and must be swallowed like a bitter pill when he goes to bed at night. 'Pon my word, that's bound in time to purge the blood and invigorate the heart! You and your like complain so much of the nobility and their arrogance and say they regard their tutors as domestic servants. You fools! What else are they, then? Are they not employed for wages and for board as servants are? But who bids you nourish their arrogance? Who bids you become domestic servants when you've acquired some learning and pledge yourselves to a pigheaded nobleman who has been accustomed all his life to a servile fawning household?

PASTOR: But Your Excellency . . . Merciful God! That's the way of the world: a man must have a vantage point from which to spy out some public office when he graduates from the university. We have to wait upon God's summons —and a patron is very often the means to our preferment. At least it was so in my case.

COUNCILLOR: Say no more, pastor, say no more, I beg of you. It does not redound to your credit. It's common knowledge, after all, that your late wife was God's summons in your case, otherwise you'd still be stuck with Herr von Tiesen and be muck-spreading on his fields. Lord! You gentry are always trying to pull some venerable wool over our eyes. There never was a nobleman took on a tutor without showing him the fair prospect of preferment beyond an avenue of eight or nine years' servitude, and when you'd gone your eight years he did like Laban and pushed the prospect back as far again. Fiddlesticks! Learn your trade and be honest men. The state will not leave you standing long in the marketplace. Honest men are needed everywhere, but rogues that simply bear the name of scholar on a tag and have their heads stuffed with empty paper . . .

PASTOR: These are very much generalities, councillor! God knows, there must be private tutors; not everyone can become a Privy Councillor straight away, even if he were a Hugo Grotius. There's more to it nowadays than simply learning.

COUNCILLOR: You grow heated, pastor! My dear, worthy pastor—let us not lose the thread of our discourse. I maintain there need not be private tutors: the vermin are not worth a tinker's damn.

PASTOR: I have not come here to listen to insults. I, too, was a private tutor. If you will excuse me . . .

COUNCILLOR: Wait a moment, do not go, my dear pastor! Heaven forbid, I did not mean to affront you, and if I did so inadvertently then I beg a thousand pardons. It's simply a bad habit of mine to get excited when a conversation interests me. I lose sight of everything else and can see nothing but the subject under discussion.

PASTOR: You are throwing—I beg your pardon, but I, too, have a hasty temper and like to speak my mind—you are throwing out the baby with the bathwater. Private tutors not worth a damn? How can you prove that? Who is to teach you young gentlemen sense and good manners? What would have become of you, Your Excellency, had you not had a private tutor?

COUNCILLOR: My father put me to the common school; I bless his memory for it, and I hope my son Fritz will one day say the same of me.

PASTOR: Yes—but there's a great deal more to be said on this subject, sir! For my part I am not of your opinion. Indeed, if the common schools were what they ought to be—but the dreary creatures who are so often in charge of the classes, the pedantic methods they employ, the evil manners current among the pupils . . .

COUNCILLOR: Whose fault is that? Who is to blame but you rascals of private tutors? If the nobleman were not encouraged by you in his foolish fancy to set up a petty court and sit like a monarch on the throne, paid homage to by tutor and governess and a rag-tag and bobtail of idle rogues, then he would have to put his youngsters to the common school. The money he now applies to having his son raised as an aristocratic blockhead he would then add to the school funds; then sensible people could be paid from these funds and everything would take its proper course. The fledgling student would be obliged to learn something in order to serve in such an institution, and as for the young gentleman, instead of hiding his indolence with artful gentility from the gaze of his papa and his aunts—who are anything but Argus-eyed—he would have to put his brains to work if he meant to outstrip the town boys and set himself apart from them. As far as manners go—they will look after themselves, although he will not learn from infancy, as his aristocratic cousins do, to stick his nose higher in the air than his fellows, to talk condescending nonsense in a drawling tone and to glare at those who raise their hats to him by way of indicating they need expect no such civility in return. The devil take fine manners! The boy may have a dancing master to visit him and be taken into polite company, but he must never on any account be singled out from the circle of his schoolmates and encouraged in the opinion that he is a better sort of creature.

PASTOR: I haven't time (*pulls out his watch*) to enter further into argument with you, Your Honor; but this much I know: the nobility are not everywhere of your opinion.

COUNCILLOR: Then the commoners should be of my opinion. Necessity would soon convince the nobility otherwise, and we could look forward to better times. Heavens above, what can become of our nobility if a single individual is to be the factotum in the education of a child? Even supposing one makes the impossible assumption that he were a man of universal scholarship, where will a single man find fire and spirit and energy if he is to focus all his powers upon a dullard, especially if father and mother meddle here, there, and everywhere in his education and keep knocking the bottom out of the barrel he's trying to fill?

PASTOR: I have an appointment with a sick parishioner at ten. You will excuse me. (*Turning back as he leaves.*) But might it not be possible, Your Honor, to board your younger son with the Major, just for six months or so? My son will gladly be satisfied with eighty ducats, but he cannot live on the sixty which Your Honor's brother means to give him.

COUNCILLOR: Let him resign. I will not do it, pastor. I will not change my mind. I'd rather make your son a present of the thirty ducats than hand my boy over to a private tutor. (*The* PASTOR *holds out a letter.*) What am I supposed to do with this? It's no use, I tell you.

PASTOR: Read it, just read it.

COUNCILLOR: Very well, you're not . . . "Do everything you can to persuade the Privy Councillor. You cannot imagine how wretchedly I am situated here; not one of the promises made to me has been kept. I dine with the family only when no visitors are present. Worst of all, I never get away from here and it's a whole year since I set foot outside Heidelbrunn. I had been promised a horse to go to Königsberg every quarter, but when I asked for it Madame inquired whether I wouldn't rather go to the carnival in Venice . . ." (*Throws the letter on the ground.*) Well, then, let him resign; why is he such a fool as to stay there?

PASTOR: That's the point. (*Picks up the letter.*) Be so kind as to read to the end of the letter.

COUNCILLOR: What is there to read? (*Reads.*) "Nevertheless I cannot leave this house, even if it should cost me my life and my health. So much I may tell you: the prospects of a blissful future to compensate for all the tribulations of my present condition . . ." Yes, prospects of a blissful eternity, otherwise I know of no prospects that my brother could offer him. He's deceiving himself, believe me: write back to him and tell him he's a fool. I'll give him a supplement of thirty ducats this year from my own purse, but I'd ask him to spare me all further soliciting regarding my Karl, for I'll not ruin my child for his sake.

SCENE TWO

Heidelbrunn. GUSTCHEN, LÄUFFER.

GUSTCHEN: What's the matter with you, then?

LÄUFFER: What about my portrait? You haven't given it a thought, have you? If I had been so negligent . . . If I'd known, I would have kept back your letter, but I was a fool.

GUSTCHEN: Ha, ha, ha! Dear Master Tutor! I really haven't had time.

LÄUFFER: Cruel girl!

GUSTCHEN: But what's the matter with you, then? Do tell me! You've never been so pensive before. Your eyes are always brimming with tears. I've noticed that you eat nothing.

LÄUFFER: Have you? Really? You are a very paragon of compassion.

GUSTCHEN: Oh, Master Tutor . . .

LÄUFFER: Do you wish to have a drawing lesson this afternoon?

GUSTCHEN: (*seizes him by the hand*): Dearest tutor! Pardon me for letting you down yesterday. I really couldn't draw: I had the most dreadful cold.

LÄUFFER: Then I expect you still have it today. I think we shall stop drawing altogether: it no longer gives you any pleasure.

GUSTCHEN (*half weeping*): How can you say that, Herr Läuffer? It's the one thing I like doing.

LÄUFFER: Or else you can put it off until the winter when you are back in town, and get yourself a drawing master. In fact I shall ask your father to remove from you the object of your loathing, your hatred, your cruelty. I can see that in the long run it will be intolerable for you to accept instruction from me.

GUSTCHEN: Herr Läuffer . . .

LÄUFFER: Leave me alone . . . I must see how I may put an end to this wretched existence, since death is forbidden me . . .

GUSTCHEN: Herr Läuffer . . .

LÄUFFER: You are torturing me. (*Tears himself away and goes off.*)

GUSTCHEN: How I pity him!

SCENE THREE

Halle, in Saxony. FRITZ VON BERG. PÄTUS *sitting at the table in his dressing gown.*

PÄTUS: I say, Berg! You're not a child any more to cry for daddy and mummy . . . Fie on you! I always took you for a stout fellow; if you weren't my old schoolmate I'd be ashamed to go about with you.

FRITZ: On my honor, Pätus, it's not homesickness. What a foolish conjecture: you make me blush to the ears! I'd gladly have news from home, I grant you, but there are reasons for that . . .

PÄTUS: Gustchen, eh? Just think, you wretched soul! A hundred and eighty hours removed from her—what forests and rivers lie between the pair of you! But wait, we have girls in Halle too. If I were only a bit more flush I'd introduce you to such company . . . I don't know what to think of you—a year in Halle and never a word to a girl: it's bound to get you down, bound to! Look, you must move in with me, that will cheer you up. What are you doing at that parson's? That's no place for you.

FRITZ: What do you pay here?

PÄTUS: I pay . . . really, brother, I don't know what I pay. My landlord's a good honest Philistine. It's true his wife's a little odd from time to time, but never mind. What does that matter to me? We have a good old squabble and I send her about her business. And they put everything on the slate—rent, coffee, tobacco, everything I ask for, and then I pay at the end of the year when my allowance arrives.

FRITZ: Do you owe much now?

PÄTUS: I settled up last week. To tell the truth they gave me a rough passage this time: my allowance is gone to the last penny, and my coat that I pawned the day before my cash arrived, because I was at the end of my tether, is still at uncle's. Heaven knows when I'll be able to get it out of hock.

FRITZ: And how do you manage now?

PÄTUS: Me? I'm sick. This morning Frau Hamster, the councillor's wife, sent me an invitation, so I crawled into bed at once . . .

FRITZ: But to sit at home in this fine weather!

PÄTUS: What does it matter? In the evenings I go for a stroll in my dressing gown; in these dog days it's beastly hot in any case during the day. God damn it! Where's my coffee? (*Stamps on the floor.*) Frau Blitzer! Now you'll see how I keep my people on the hop. Frau Blitzer! Where the devil . . . Frau Blitzer! (*Rings the bell and thumps on the floor.*) I've only just paid her: I can afford to take a strong line! Frau . . . (FRAU BLITZER *enters with coffee.*)

PÄTUS: Where the devil were you, Frau Blitzer? A plague on you, I've been waiting over an hour . . .

FRAU BLITZER: What? What's all this row for, you good-for-nothing? Broke again, are you, you threadbare louse? I'll take my coffee back again this instant . . .

PÄTUS (*pours out coffee*): Now, now, don't be so ill-tempered, Mother Blitzer! But the cookies—where are the cookies?

FRAU BLITZER: Balls to you! There's not a cookie in the house. D'you think a bare-arsed lousy fellow like you should eat cookies every afternoon?

PÄTUS: Damn it all! (*Stamps his foot.*) You know I never drink a mouthful of coffee without cookies! What am I paying all that money for?

FRAU BLITZER (*taking cookies out of her apron pocket and pulling his hair*): Look, here's your cookies, loudmouth! He's got a voice like a whole regiment of soldiers! Well, is the coffee good? Or isn't it? Tell me this minute or I'll tear the last of your hair out of that bald pate of yours.

PÄTUS (*drinks*): Matchless—Ow! Never drank a better in my life.

FRAU BLITZER: You see, you dog! If you didn't have Mother Blitzer to look after you and give you food and drink, you'd starve in the street. Just look at him, Herr von Berg, the way he goes around, no coat to his back and his dressing gown looks as if he'd been hanged in it and fallen off the gallows. You're a pretty gentleman, I don't know how you can have anything to do with him. Well, I suppose you're a fellow countryman of his, and blood's thicker than water, that's what I always say, and if only Herr von Berg would come and lodge with us . . . I know you have influence over him: you might make something of him yet, but otherwise, to tell the truth . . . (*Exit.*)

PÄTUS: See, isn't she a jolly old girl? I turn a blind eye mostly, but dammit, if I once take it seriously she's as meek as that wall there. Will you take a cup with me? (*Pours out a cup of coffee for* FRITZ.) You see, I'm well looked after here; I pay a pretty fair price, but at least I get something in return . . .

FRITZ (*drinks*): This coffee tastes of barley.

PÄTUS: What d'you say? (*Tastes it.*) Yes, it's true; what with the cookie, I didn't . . . (*Looks into the pot.*) To hell with it! (*Throws the pot out of the window.*) Barley coffee and 500 gulden a year!

FRAU BLITZER (*rushes in*): Hey! What the devil's this? Are you crazy, or has the devil himself got into you?

PÄTUS: Quiet, Mother Blitzer!

FRAU BLITZER (*screaming at the top of her voice*): Where's my coffee service? Out of the window? What the hell! I'll scratch your eyes out, you!

PÄTUS: There was a spider in the pot and I got such a fright I flung it away—is it my fault the window was open?

FRAU BLITZER: I wish you'd choked to death on your spider: if I sell you up neck and crop it won't pay for my coffeepot, you worthless hound! Nothing but breakages and calamities, that's all you're fit for. I'll have the law on you, I'll have you thrown in jail. (*Rushes off.*)

PÄTUS (*laughing*): What can we do, brother? She must just have her rage out.

FRITZ: But at your expense?

PÄTUS: So what! If I have to wait until Christmas, who'll give me credit that long? And, anyway, she's only a woman, and a foolish one at that; she doesn't always mean it. If it had been her husband that would have been another matter; I'd have given him a good thrashing, see?

FRITZ: Do you have pen and ink?

PÄTUS: There, on the windowsill.

FRITZ: I can't think why, but I feel so downhearted—I've never taken much notice of forebodings.

PÄTUS: I feel the same. Döbblin's company has come to town. I'd like to go to the play and I haven't a coat to put on. My scoundrelly landlord won't lend me one, and I'm such a great fat beast not one of yours will fit me.

FRITZ: I must write home straight away. (*Sits down by the window and begins to write.*)

PÄTUS (*sits down facing a wolfskin coat hanging on the wall*): Hm! Nothing but that wolfskin rescued from all the clothes I had or meant to have made. It would have to be the wolf-skin, of all things, that I can't wear in summer and that the Jew won't take in pledge because the moth gets into it so easily. Hanke, Hanke! It's a scandal you won't make me a coat on tick! (*Stands up and walks about the room.*) What have I done to you, Hanke, that you won't make a coat for me, of all people? Me, of all people, who needs one most of all, because I don't possess one, why pick on me? Devil take you, you give credit to every Tom, Dick, or Harry, but not to me! (*Clutches his head and stamps on the floor.*) Me of all people! Me, of all people!

BOLLWERK (*who has crept in meanwhile and has been listening to* PÄTUS, *grabs hold of him;* PÄTUS *turns round and stands in front of* BOLLWERK *without speaking*): Ha, ha, ha! . . . Poor Pätus! . . . Ha, ha, ha! Isn't he a godless fellow, Hanke —for you of all people . . . But where's the scarlet suit with gold trimmings you ordered from him, and the blue silk with silver embroidered waistcoat, and the red velvet lined with black velvet—just the thing for this time of year? Tell me! Answer me! That confounded fellow Hanke! Shall we go and give him a thrashing? What's he doing with your order all this time? Shall we?

PÄTUS (*throws himself into a chair*): Leave me alone.

BOLLWERK: But listen, Pätus, Pätus, Pä-, Pä-, Pä-, Pätus (*Sits down beside him.*) Döbblin has arrived. Listen, Pä-, Pä-, Pä-, Pä-, Pätus, how shall we manage? I think you ought to put on your wolfskin coat and go to the play. What's the harm, no one knows you here—and everybody knows you've ordered four suits of clothes from Hanke. Whether he'll make them or not, doesn't matter! Confounded fellow! We'll smash his windows if he doesn't make them for you!

PÄTUS (*violently*): Leave me alone, I tell you!

BOLLWERK: But listen . . . but . . . but . . . but . . . list . . . list . . . listen, Pätus. Watch out, Pätus, that you don't go running around the streets in your dressing gown at nights again. I know you're scared of dogs; the town crier has just announced there are ten mad dogs loose in town. They've bitten some children already: two of them recovered but four died on the spot. It's because of the dog days! Isn't it, Pätus? It's a good thing you can't go out, isn't it? You'll take care not to go out, won't you, Pä-, Pä-, Pätus?

PÄTUS: Leave me alone—or else we shall fall out.

BOLLWERK: Don't be such a child. Berg, will you come to the play with me?

FRITZ (*absent-mindedly*): What? What play?

BOLLWERK: Some actors have come to town. Stop your scribbling. You can do your writing this evening. They're doing *Minna von Barnhelm* today.

FRITZ: Oh, I must see that. (*Puts away his letters.*) Poor old Pätus, you haven't a coat to wear.

BOLLWERK: I'd gladly lend him one, but, Devil take it, this is the only one I've got to my back. (FRITZ *and* BOLLWERK *exeunt.*)

PÄTUS: To the Devil with you two and your pity! It rankles more than a slap in the face. Oh, what do I care. (*Pulls off his dressing gown.*) Let people think I'm crazy! I must see *Minna von Barnhelm*, even if I have to go stark naked! (*Puts on the wolfskin coat.*) Hanke, Hanke! A plague on you! (*Stamps his foot.*) A plague on you and yours! (*Exit.*)

SCENE FOUR

FRAU HAMSTER, FRÄULEIN HAMSTER, FRÄULEIN KNICKS.

FRÄULEIN KNICKS: I can hardly tell you of it for laughing, Frau Hamster. I've nearly laughed myself sick. Just imagine: we were going down the lane just here with Fräulein Hamster when a man in a wolfskin coat came rushing past us as if he were running the gauntlet, with three huge dogs hard on his heels. Fräulein Hamster got such a buffet she banged her head on the wall and couldn't help screaming at the top of her voice.

FRAU HAMSTER: Who was it, then?

FRÄULEIN KNICKS: Just imagine, when we looked round, it was Herr Pätus. He must have gone crazy.

FRAU HAMSTER: A wolfskin coat in this heat!

FRÄULEIN HAMSTER (*holding her head*): I still think he jumped out of bed in a raging fever. He sent us a message this morning that he was sick.

FRÄULEIN KNICKS: And the three dogs hard on his heels, that was the funniest part. I meant to go to the play today, but I'd rather not now, I'd not have half as much to laugh at there. I'll never forget it as long as I live. His hair was streaming out behind him like the tail of a comet, and the faster he ran the more the dogs barked, and he hadn't even the heart to look round . . . It was priceless!

FRAU HAMSTER: Didn't he shout? He must have thought the dogs were mad.

FRÄULEIN KNICKS: I don't believe he had time to shout, but he was as red as a lobster and had his mouth wide open, and what with the dogs at his heels—Oh, it was quite priceless! I'd have given my string of real pearls not to have missed it.

SCENE FIVE

Heidelbrunn. GUSTCHEN's *room.* GUSTCHEN *is lying on the bed,* LÄUFFER *is sitting beside her.*

LÄUFFER: Imagine, Gustchen, the Privy Councillor refuses to do it. You can see your father is making my life more and more of a misery: now he proposes to give me no more than forty ducats for the coming year. How can I put up with that? I shall have to quit.

GUSTCHEN: Cruel man! What shall I do then? (*After they have looked at each other in silence for a moment.*) You can see: I am weak and sick, all alone here in the power of a brutal mother. No one asks after me, no one bothers about me. No one in my whole family cares for me any more, not even father. I don't know why.

LÄUFFER: Make them send you to be taught by my father in Insterburg.

GUSTCHEN: We would never see each other there. My uncle would never allow father to put me in your father's house.

LÄUFFER: Beastly snobbery!

GUSTCHEN (*takes his hand*): If you get angry too, my sweet Herrmann! (*Kisses his hand.*) Oh, death! Death! Why dost thou not take pity on me?

LÄUFFER: All right, you tell me what to do. Your brother is the most ill-bred youth I've ever known. The other day he boxed my ears and I dared not lay a finger on him in return, dared not even complain. Your father would have broken every bone in his body, and your respected mama would have put the blame on me in the end.

GUSTCHEN: But for my sake. I thought you loved me.

LÄUFFER (*leans on the bed with one hand while she continues to put his other hand to her lips from time to time*): Let me think . . . (*Sits plunged in thought.*)

GUSTCHEN (*carrying on her act as above*): Oh, Romeo! If this were but thy hand! But thou dost leave me thus, ignoble Romeo! Dost thou not see that thy Juliet expires for thee, by all the world, by all her kin abhorred, despised, spat out! (*Presses his hand to her eyes.*) Oh, inhuman Romeo!

LÄUFFER: What are you raving about now?

GUSTCHEN: It's a monologue from a tragedy that I like to recite when I have cares. (LÄUFFER *is again plunged in thought; after a pause she begins again.*) Perhaps thou art not so culpable. Thy father's prohibition on exchanging letters; but love leaps over seas and rivers, over prohibitions and even over mortal perils. Thou hast forgot me . . . Perhaps thy concern for me . . . yes, yes, thy tender heart conceived the things that threatened me as more fearsome than my present suffering. (*Kisses* LÄUFFER's *hand ardently*.) Oh, divine Romeo!

LÄUFFER (*presses a long kiss on her hand and looks at her for a while in silence*): I might suffer the same fate as Abelard ...

GUSTCHEN (*sits up*): You are mistaken. My sickness is in the mind. No one will suppose you ... (*Falls back*.) Have you read *La nouvelle Héloïse*?

LÄUFFER: I can hear someone in the passage to the school-room ...

GUSTCHEN: Father—for heaven's sake! You've spent three quarters of an hour too long with me. (LÄUFFER *rushes off*.)

SCENE SIX

The MAJOR'S WIFE, COUNT VERMOUTH.

COUNT: But dearest lady! May one never hope to set eyes upon Fräulein Gustchen again? How was she after the hunt the other day?

MAJOR'S WIFE: If it please you, she had toothache during the night, that's why she cannot make her appearance today. How is your digestion, Count, after the oysters?

COUNT: Oh, I'm used to that. Not long ago my brother and I between us ate six hundred oysters and washed them down with twenty bottles of champagne.

MAJOR'S WIFE: Hock, you mean.

COUNT: Champagne—it was just an idea we had, and it did us not the slightest harm. The same evening there was a ball in Königsberg; my brother danced until noon the following day while I was busy losing money.

MAJOR'S WIFE: Shall we have a hand of piquet?

COUNT: If Fräulein Gustchen came down I would take a turn in the garden with her. I would not presume to invite you to do the same, dear lady, on account of the ulcer on your foot.

MAJOR'S WIFE: I can't think where the Major has got to. In all his life he's never been so mad on farming: out in the fields every minute of the day, and when he does come home he

sits there as dumb as a post. Believe me, it's beginning to
make me think.

COUNT: He seems melancholic.

MAJOR'S WIFE: Heaven knows—not long ago he took it into
his head to sleep with me again, and what if he didn't
leap out of bed in the middle of the night and (*she giggles*)
—I ought not to tell you, really, but you know my husband's
comic side well enough.

COUNT: And . . . ?

MAJOR'S WIFE: Flung himself down on his knees and beat his
breast and sobbed and howled—it was enough to make my
blood run cold. But I didn't care to ask him why; what are
his foolish pranks to me? Let him turn Pietist or Quaker
for all I care! It makes him no more odious to me—or more
attractive—than he already is. (*Casts a coquettish look at
the* COUNT.)

COUNT (*takes hold of her chin*): Wicked woman! But where is
Gustchen? I'd love to take a stroll with her.

MAJOR'S WIFE: Hush, here's the Major . . . You can go for a
stroll with him, Count.

COUNT: I say . . . but I want to go for a walk with your
daughter.

MAJOR'S WIFE: She'll not be dressed yet: insufferable, how
idle the girl is . . .

(*The* MAJOR *enters wearing a nightshirt and a straw hat.*)

MAJOR'S WIFE: Well, how goes it, husband? Where have you
been all this time? We never set eyes on you from one day's
end to the other. Look at him, Count. He looks like the
picture of Heautontimorumenos in my big Dacier. I
believe you've been plowing, Major? We're in the dog days
now, you know.

COUNT: Indeed, Major, you've never looked so ill, so pale and
haggard; you must have something on your mind. What's
the meaning of these tears that spring to your eyes as soon
as anyone looks closely at you? I've known you now for ten
years and never seen you so, not even when your brother
died.

MAJOR'S WIFE: Stinginess, nothing but cursed stinginess; he
thinks we'll starve if he doesn't keep grubbing in the fields

every day like a mole. When he's not digging or plowing he's harrowing. You surely don't mean to turn peasant? You'll need to give me another man first to keep an eye on you.

MAJOR: I've got to toil and scrape to get my daughter a place in the hospital.

MAJOR'S WIFE: Not these fantasies again! I really must call Doctor Würz from Königsberg.

MAJOR: You have eyes for nothing, grand lady that you are! Your child is wasting away from day to day, losing her looks, her health, and all the rest, and drifting around as if—Devil take it, and may God forgive me the sin—as if poor Lazarus had made her. In truth, it cuts me to the quick.

MAJOR'S WIFE: Listen to him! How he flies out at me! Am I to blame? Are you crazy?

MAJOR: Indeed you are to blame, what else is to blame? Damn it, I cannot understand it. I always thought I'd arrange the finest match in the whole empire for her, for there was no one in the whole wide world to equal her for looks—and now she looks like a milkmaid. Yes, indeed, you're to blame with your strictness and your cruelties and your jealousy, she's taken it all to heart and now it shows in her face, but that's a joy to you, madam, because you've been jealous of her for long enough. You can't deny that, can you? You should think burning shame of yourself 'pon my word! (*Exit.*)

MAJOR'S WIFE: But . . . but what do you say to that, Count? Have you ever heard such a deal of nonsense in all your life?

COUNT: Come, let us play a hand of piquet until Fräulein Gustchen has finished dressing . . .

SCENE SEVEN

Halle. FRITZ VON BERG *in prison,* BOLLWERK, SEIFFENBLASE, *and* SEIFFENBLASE'S TUTOR *standing round him.*

BOLLWERK: If I had the lad here I'd skin him alive. After all it's a scurrilous trick to land an honest chap like Berg in jail—and no one to take his part. For one thing is certainly

true: not one of his countrymen has stirred outside his door
to help him. If Berg had not gone bail for him, he'd have
rotted in jail. The money is supposed to be here in two
weeks, and if he leaves Berg in a fix, then he's nothing but
an out-and-out villain. Oh, you cursed Pä-, Pä-, Pä-,
Pätus! Just wait, you gallows bird Pätus, just you wait!

TUTOR: I cannot tell you, dear Herr von Berg, how sorry I
am, particularly for the sake of your respected father and
your family, to see you in this condition, and through no
fault of your own at that, but simply through youthful
folly. One of the seven wise men of Greece once said, thou
shalt beware of standing surety, and indeed nothing is
more scandalous than that a young wastrel, who has
plunged himself into penury by riotous living, should drag
others down with him, for presumably that was what he
had in mind from the start when he sought your friendship
at college.

SEIFFENBLASE: Yes, yes, brother Berg, you won't mind my
saying so, but you've made a downright blunder. It's all
your own fault; you might have known the moment you
clapped eyes on the fellow that he'd do you down. He came
to me as well and spun his yarn: he was at the end of his
tether, his creditors meant to put him behind bars. Let
them, thought I, it'll do you no harm. Serve you right:
you haven't a kind look for us, but when you're in trouble
then your aristocratic friends are good enough to serve as
guarantors. He told me this, that, and the other: he had
loaded his pistols in case his creditors fell upon him . . . And
now the dissolute dog uses you so! To be frank, if it had
happened to me I could not take it so calmly: Herr von
Berg locked up, and all for the sake of a wastrel student!

FRITZ: He was my schoolmate . . . Leave him alone. If I
don't complain of him, what's it to you? I've known him
longer than the lot of you; I know he wouldn't leave me
sitting here if he could help it.

TUTOR: But Herr von Berg, we must act sensibly in this world.
It does him no harm to have you sitting here in place of
him, and for all he cares you may sit here for a century
yet . . .

FRITZ: I've known him since we were children: we have never yet refused each other anything. He loved me like his own brother, as I did him. When he went away to Halle he wept for the first time in his life because we weren't to go together. He could have gone to college a whole year earlier but so as to go with me he pretended to the examiners that he was duller than he really was, and still fate and our fathers decreed that we should not go together, and that was his undoing. He never could handle money and simply gave everyone whatever he asked for. If a beggar had snatched the last shirt off his back and said: By your leave, dear Herr Pätus, he'd have let it go. His creditors have treated him like footpads, and his father never deserved to have a prodigal son who, for all his poverty, brought home such a sterling heart.

TUTOR: Pardon me, but you're young and see everything from the most favorable angle: you need to have lived a long while among men in order to judge of their character. Herr Pätus, or whatever his name is, has shown himself to you so far in a false guise; this is the first time his true face has come to light: he must have been one of the most subtle and wily deceivers, for honest rogues . . .

PÄTUS (*in traveling garb, enters and throws his arms around* BERG's *neck*): Brother Berg . . .

FRITZ: Brother Pätus . . .

PÄTUS: No . . . leave me . . . I must lie here at your feet . . . you in this place . . . on my account! (*Tears his hair with both hands and stamps his feet.*) Oh, destiny, destiny, destiny!

FRITZ: Well, how goes it? Have you brought some money with you? Have you made it up with your father? What brings you back here?

PÄTUS: Nothing, nothing . . . He refused to see me . . . a hundred miles, and all for nothing! Your servant, gentlemen. Do not weep, Bollwerk, you humble me if you think well of me. Heavens, heavens!

FRITZ: Then you're the greatest fool to walk the earth. Why did you come back? Are you crazy? Have you taken leave of your senses? Do you want your creditors to see you? Get out! Bollwerk, take him away; see that you get him

safely out of town. I can hear the beadle coming . . . Pätus,
you're my enemy for life if you don't this instant . . .
(PÄTUS *falls at* FRITZ's *feet.*)

FRITZ: You'll drive me out of my mind!

BOLLWERK: Don't be such an idiot when Berg is noble enough
to sit here in your place. His father will bail him out, but
if you once land in here there's not a hope for you: you'll
rot in jail.

PÄTUS: Give me a sword . . .

FRITZ: Get out!

BOLLWERK: Get out!

PÄTUS: Have pity on me and give me a sword!

SEIFFENBLASE: Here, have mine.

BOLLWERK: (*seizes* SEIFFENBLASE's *arm*): You scoundrel, sir!
Stop, don't put up your blade! You shan't have drawn in
vain. First I'll see my friend safely out of here, but you may
expect me back—outside, of course. But the first thing is to
get out of here! (*Pushes* SEIFFENBLASE *out.*)

TUTOR: Herr Bollwerk!

BOLLWERK: Not a word, you! Get after your boy and teach
him not to be a cad . . . I'm at your service anywhere you
want and any time you wish.

PÄTUS: Bollwerk, I'll be your second!

BOLLWERK: You're an idiot too! Would you care to hold my
glove while I take a piss beforehand? Who needs seconds?
Come on then and get yourself seconded out of town, you
funk!

PÄTUS: But there are two of them.

BOLLWERK: I only wish there were ten of them and not a
Seiffenblase among them. Come on, unless you want to
ruin yourself, you ass.

PÄTUS: Berg! (BOLLWERK *drags him away.*)

ACT THREE

SCENE ONE

Heidelbrunn. The MAJOR *in his nightshirt,*
the PRIVY COUNCILLOR.

MAJOR: I'm not the man I was, brother. If you could see my
heart you'd find it's ten times crazier than my face. It's a
very good thing you've come to visit me, who knows
whether we'll be able to see each other much longer.

COUNCILLOR: You exaggerate in everything—taking such a
trifle to heart like this! Even if your daughter loses her
looks she's still the good girl she always was: she may still
possess a hundred other amiable qualities.

MAJOR: Her looks? Devil take me, that's not all she's lost! I
don't know, I think I'll lose my wits if I have to look at the
girl much longer. Her health is gone, her high spirits, her
charm, damn it, whatever you care to call it; but even if I
can't put a name to it I can see it, feel it, and understand
it, and you know I idolized the girl. And to see her fade
away under my hands, to see her decay . . . (*Weeps.*)
Brother Councillor, you have no daughter, you don't know
how a father must feel who has a daughter. I've been in
thirteen battles and suffered eighteen wounds and looked
death in the face and I'm . . . Oh, leave me alone, clear off
out of my house, let the whole world clear off. I'll set the
world on fire, take my shovel in my hand and turn peasant.

COUNCILLOR: And your wife and children?

MAJOR: You must be joking: I know nothing of wife and
children, I'm Major Berg of blessed memory, and I'll put
my hand to the plow and become Father Berg, and anyone

who comes too near me shall have my mattock about his ears.

COUNCILLOR: I've never known him rave so wildly in his melancholy fits.

(*The* MAJOR'S WIFE *rushes in.*)

MAJOR'S WIFE: Help, husband! We're ruined! Our family! Our family!

COUNCILLOR: God forbid, sister! What's all this to-do? Would you drive your husband mad?

MAJOR'S WIFE: He shall go mad. Our family . . . infamous! Oh, I am undone! (*Falls into a chair.*)

MAJOR (*goes up to her*): Will you speak plain? Or must I wring your neck!

MAJOR'S WIFE: Your daughter . . . the tutor . . . go quickly! (*Faints.*)

MAJOR: Has he made a whore of her? (*Shakes his wife.*) Why must you faint, this is no time to faint. Made a whore of her, is that it? Then let the whole world turn whore and you, Berg, take up your pitchfork . . . (*Makes to go off.*)

COUNCILLOR (*holds the* MAJOR *back*): Brother, if you love your life, stay where you are. I'll see to everything; you're mad with fury and not accountable for your actions. (*Exit, locking the door behind him.*)

MAJOR (*wrestling with the door in vain*): I'll give you "accountable"! (*To his wife.*) Come, come, whore that you are! Watch me! (*Tears open the door.*) I'll make an example . . . God has spared me until this moment so that I can make an example of wife and children! Burn, burn, burn! (*Drags off his unconscious wife.*)

SCENE TWO

A village school on a dark evening.
WENZESLAUS, LÄUFFER.

WENZESLAUS (*sitting at a table, spectacles on his nose, drawing lines in exercise books*): Who's there? What's to do?

LÄUFFER: Save me! Save me, worthy schoolmaster! They're out to kill me!

WENZESLAUS: Who are you, then?

LÄUFFER: I'm the tutor at the manor here. Major Berg is after me with all his servants, and they mean to shoot me.

WENZESLAUS: Heaven forbid! Sit ye down beside me. Here's my hand. You're safe enough with me. And now tell me all about it while I do these copybooks.

LÄUFFER: First let me pull myself together.

WENZESLAUS: All right, get your breath back, and then I'll see you have a glass of wine and we'll drink together. Meanwhile, tell me then—tutor—(*Puts down his ruler, takes off his glasses and gazes at* LÄUFFER *for a while.*) Well, judging by your coat ... There now, I'll believe you're a tutor. You've got a pink and white look about you. But do tell me, my dear friend, (*puts his glasses on again*) how were you so ill-starred as to incur your employer's wrath? I simply cannot imagine that a man like Major von Berg—I know him well, he has a hasty temper: most choleric, most choleric ... Look, I have to draw the lines myself for the boys, because the lads find nothing so difficult to learn as writing straight, writing evenly. Not neat writing, not rapid writing, I always say, but straight writing, because that affects everything—morals, the sciences, everything, my dear tutor. A man who can't write straight, I always say, can't act straight ... where were we?

LÄUFFER: Might I ask you for a glass of water?

WENZESLAUS: Water? You shall have it. But ... what were we speaking about just now? Writing straight—no, about the major, hum, hum, hum! But do you know, Herr ... What is your name?

LÄUFFER: My ...? My name is—Mandel.

WENZESLAUS: Herr Mandel ... and you had to think about it? Oh, well, people are sometimes absent-minded, especially pink and white young gentlemen. Mandel's not a proper name for you: you should be called Mandelblüte, because you're as pink and white as almond blossom. Well, indeed, the condition of a private tutor is amongst those, *unus ex his*, that are perpetually strewn with roses and lilies and where the thorns of life most rarely prick. For what have you to do? You eat, drink, sleep, you haven't a care in the world; a good glass of wine for sure, a roast each day, every morning your coffee, tea, chocolate, or whatever you drink, and so it goes on. Now then, I meant to tell you: do you know, Herr Mandel, that a glass of water on top of a violent effervescence of the passions can be as harmful to your health as after violent physical exercise? But, there, what do you young gentlemen tutors ever care for your health. Tell me, then, (*puts down his ruler and glasses and stands up*) how on earth can it possibly be good for your health if all your nerves and arteries are tense and your blood is in the most rapid circulation and the vital spirits are all in— an excitation, in—

LÄUFFER: For heaven's sake! Count Vermouth! (*Dives into the bedroom.*)

(COUNT VERMOUTH *enters with a number of servants carrying pistols.*)

COUNT VERMOUTH: Is there someone called Läuffer here, a student in a blue brocaded coat?

WENZESLAUS: Sir, in our village it's customary for a man to take off his hat when he comes into the room and addresses the master of the house.

COUNT VERMOUTH: We're in a hurry. Tell me, is he here or isn't he?

WENZESLAUS: And what crime has he committed that you are looking for him with firearms in your hands? (*The* COUNT *tries to enter the bedroom;* WENZESLAUS *takes up his stance in front of the door.*) Stop sir! That's my room, and if you don't clear out of my house this minute I'll ring my bell and half-a-dozen sturdy farmlads will smash you to smithereens. If you are highwaymen then you must be treated like highwaymen. And to make sure you don't get lost and fail to find your way out of the house as easily as you found your way in . . . (*Seizes his hand and leads him out of the door; the servants follow.*)

LÄUFFER (*rushes out of the bedroom*): Oh, happy man! Enviable man!

WENZESLAUS (*resumes his former attitude*): In . . . er . . . the vital spirits, as I was saying, are in an excitation, all the passions, as it were, in a flurry and turmoil. Now, if you drink water, it's like pouring water on a fierce flame. The violent motion of the air and the conflict between the opposing elements creates an effervescence, a fermentation, a commotion, a turbulent condition . . .

LÄUFFER: I admire you . . .

WENZESLAUS (*calling his servant*): Gottlieb! Now you may drink, but take it slowly—slowly—and then you can make the best of a sausage and salad for supper. What sort of uncivil fellow was that who was looking for you?

LÄUFFER: It's Count Vermouth, the Major's intended son-in-law. He's jealous of me because the young lady can't abide him . . .

WENZESLAUS: What's all this, then? What does the girl want with a young ladykiller like you? Ruin her fortune for the sake of a young Siegfried with neither hearth nor home to his name? Put that out of your head and follow me into the kitchen. I see the lad has gone to fetch my sausages. I'll draw you some water myself because I haven't a maid and I haven't yet dared even to think of a wife because I know I can't afford to feed one—never mind casting covetous eyes on one, like you young pink and white gentlemen. But they say the world is changing, and I dare say they're right.

SCENE THREE

Heidelbrunn. The PRIVY COUNCILLOR,
HERR VON SEIFFENBLASE, *and* SEIFFENBLASE'S TUTOR.

TUTOR: We spent only a year in Halle, and when we came back from Göttingen we traveled via all the celebrated universities of Germany. So we couldn't spend long in Halle the second time we were there. In any case, your son, I am sorry to say, happened to be in custody at that very time, so I did not have the honor of conversing with him more than once or twice. To be frank, therefore, I would be unable to give you any very exact account of your son's behavior in foreign parts.

COUNCILLOR: Heaven sees fit to chastise our whole family. My brother—I will not attempt to keep it from you, for, alas, it's all over the town and the countryside round about —my brother has had the misfortune to lose his daughter, who has vanished without trace. And now I have such news of my son. If he had behaved himself properly, how could he possibly have been thrown into prison? Apart from a hefty monthly allowance I sent him something extra every six months or so. In any case . . .

TUTOR: Evil company, the astounding temptations in our colleges.

SEIFFENBLASE: The oddest thing is, he's in jail in place of someone else, a monster of moral laxity, a man to whom I wouldn't give a farthing, even if he were starving on a midden. He has been here, you will have heard of him, seeking money from his father on the pretext of bailing out your son; presumably he would have gone to another university with it and begun his old manner of life all over again. I know how these depraved students carry on, but his father smelled a rat and declined to see him.

COUNCILLOR: You don't mean young Pätus, the alderman's son?

SEIFFENBLASE: I believe it is the same.

COUNCILLOR: We all deplored his father's harshness.

TUTOR: What is there to deplore, Your Excellency? If a son abuses his father's kindness, then naturally his father's heart will turn against him. The high priest Eli was not harsh, and he broke his neck.

COUNCILLOR: No one can possibly be too harsh concerning his children's excesses, but he may well be so in regard to their distresses. They say the young man had to beg his living here. And my son is in prison for his sake?

SEIFFENBLASE: What else? He was the man's closest friend and found no one worthier with whom to act the comedy of Damon and Pythias. What's more, Herr Pätus went back and sought to take his rightful place again, but your son insisted he would stay where he was: you would shortly bail him out. And Pätus, along with another arch-braggart and gambler, meant to decamp, and they proposed to make their way in the world as best they could. Perhaps they will mask themselves and fall upon some wretched student in his lodgings and take his watch and his purse at pistol point, as has already happened to someone in Halle.

COUNCILLOR: And my son is the third in this unholy trio?

SEIFFENBLASE: That I cannot say, Councillor.

COUNCILLOR: Come and dine with me, gentlemen! I have heard too much already. There is a judgment of God on certain families: some have hereditary diseases, in others the children go to the bad, whatever the fathers may do. Eat your fill: I will fast and pray. It may be that this evening is the retribution for my dissolute youth.

SCENE FOUR

The schoolhouse. WENZESLAUS *and* LÄUFFER
eating at a bare table.

WENZESLAUS: How do you like it? A world of difference, isn't there, between my table and the Major's? But when Schoolmaster Wenzeslaus eats his sausage his digestion is promoted by a clear conscience, and when Herr Mandel ate his roast capon with mushroom sauce his conscience well-nigh made him choke on every morsel. You're a . . . Tell me, then, my dear Herr Mandel, you will not take it amiss if I speak plain: that lends savor to conversation like pepper in a cucumber salad—tell me, isn't it a rascally trick, if I'm convinced I'm an ignoramus and incapable of teaching my charges anything, and so idle away my time, and let them idle too and fritter away God's good time, and yet have a hundred ducats . . . or wasn't it so much? May God forgive me, I've never clapped eyes on so much money all at once in all my life! To put a hundred and fifty ducats in my pocket, I say, for nothing, absolutely nothing!

LÄUFFER: Oh, that's not half the story by any means, you don't know how lucky you are—or you simply sense it without realizing it. Have you never seen a slave in a braided coat? Oh, freedom, golden freedom!

WENZESLAUS: Freedom, my foot! I'm not as free as all that either. I'm tied to my school and accountable for it to God and my conscience.

LÄUFFER: That's just it! But supposing you were accountable to the whims of a giddy mind that treated you a hundred times worse than you treated your scholars?

WENZESLAUS: Well, yes—but then he'd have to be as far superior to me in intelligence as I am superior to my scholars, and that's not something you'll often come across, I don't believe, especially among the sprigs of our nobility. You may well be right: at least as regards the lout who tried to force his way into my bedroom just now without asking my permission. If I went to the Count and tried to search his rooms without as much as a by-your-leave . . . But, bless my soul, eat up; you're pulling faces as if you were supping a laxative. You'd like a glass of wine with it, wouldn't you? It's true I promised you one just now, but I've none in the house. I'll get some tomorrow, and we'll drink on Sundays and Thursdays and also when Franz the organist comes to visit us. Water, water, my friend, *ariston men to hudor*, that's what I learned at school, and to smoke a pipe after meals and to take a stroll round the fields in the moonlight, then you'll sleep more soundly than the Grand Mogul. You'll join me in a pipe today?

LÄUFFER: I'll try it: I've never smoked in my life.

WENZESLAUS: Yes, to be sure, you pink and white gentlemen, it ruins your teeth, doesn't it? And spoils the complexion, eh? I took up smoking when I was scarcely weaned from my mother's breast: exchanged her nipple for the butt of a pipe. Hum, hum, hum! It's good against foul air—and against foul lusts as well. That's my daily diet: cold water and a pipe of a morning, then school until eleven, then another pipe until the broth is ready—my Gottlieb cooks it as well as any of your French chefs—and a roast and a few vegetables to go with it and then another pipe, then school once more, then copybooks until suppertime. I usually eat something cold then, a sausage with salad, a piece of cheese or whatever the good Lord has given me, and then a pipe before I go to bed.

LÄUFFER: Heaven help me, I've landed up in a smokeroom . . .

WENZESLAUS: And I grow fat on it and enjoy life and do not mean to die yet a while.

LÄUFFER: It's a disgrace that your superiors never think of making your life more comfortable.

WENZESLAUS: Oh, well, that's the way it is, and one has to put up with it. At least I'm my own master, and no one has any call to order me about, because I know all along that I'm doing more than I'm obliged to. I'm supposed to teach my boys reading and writing: I teach them sums as well, and Latin, and I teach them to read sensibly into the bargain, and to write things that are worthwhile.

LÄUFFER: And what sort of reward do you get for it?

WENZESLAUS: What sort of reward? Wouldn't you like to eat up that tiny little piece of sausage? You'll get nothing better; otherwise you'll have to go hungry to bed for the first time in your life. What sort of reward? That was a foolish question, Herr Mandel, if you'll excuse my saying so. What sort of reward? God's reward is what I have, and a clear conscience, and if I were to ask a larger reward of my superiors, then I should lose the reward I have. Do you really mean to let the cucumber salad go to waste? Eat up! Don't be coy: there's no point in being coy with such short commons. Wait, I'll cut you another slice of bread.

LÄUFFER: I've had my fill and more.

WENZESLAUS: Well, leave it then, but it's your own fault if it isn't the truth. And if it is the truth, then you're wrong to eat more than your fill, because it rouses evil lusts and lulls the mind to sleep—whether you pink and white gentlemen believe it or not. I'll grant they say of tobacco, too, that it possesses a narcotic, soporific, stupefying oil, and I've found at times that it's true and have been tempted to throw my pipe and the rest of the rubbish into the fire, but the fogs we have constantly around here and the damp air in winter and autumn all the time, and the splendid effect it has on me and the fact that it lulls evil lusts to sleep as well . . . Hello, where are you then, my dear man? The very moment I talk of lulling to sleep you start to nod. That's what happens when your head is empty and idle and has never known hard work. *Allons!* Come, smoke a pipe with me! (*Fills pipes for himself and* LÄUFFER.) Let's go on chatting for a bit! (*Smoking.*) I meant to say to you in the kitchen a moment ago that I see you're weak in Latin, but since you write a fair hand, by your own account, you could help me out in the evenings writing copybooks for the boys, because I must start to spare my eyes. I'll let you have Corderius' *Colloquia* and Gürtler's *Lexicon* if you have a mind to be diligent. After all, you have the whole day to yourself, you can brush up your Latin, and who knows when it will please God to take me from this world, today or tomorrow maybe . . . But you must work hard, I tell you, for at the moment you're scarcely fit to be an assistant, never mind a . . . (*Drinks.*)

LÄUFFER (*puts down his pipe*): How humiliating!

WENZESLAUS: But . . . but . . . but . . . (*Snatches a toothpick from* LÄUFFER's *mouth.*) What's this, then? Haven't you even learned, grown man that you are, to look after your own body? Picking your teeth is suicide. Yes, suicide, a wanton destruction of Jerusalem practiced on your teeth. Here, if something's stuck in your teeth. (*Takes water and rinses his mouth.*) That's how you must do it, if you want to keep healthy teeth to the glory of God and your fellow men, and not run around in your old age like an old dog on a chain whose teeth were pulled when he was young and who cannot keep his jaws together. A fine schoolmaster he'll turn out, God willing, if the words fall stillborn from his lips and he snorts out between his nose and upper lip something that neither man nor beast can understand.

LÄUFFER: He'll schoolmaster me to death—and the worst of it is, he's right.

WENZESLAUS: Well, how goes it? Don't you care for the tobacco? A few more days with old Wenzeslaus and we'll have you smoking like any Jack Tar. I'll take you in hand so you won't know yourself in the end.

ACT FOUR

SCENE ONE

Insterburg. PRIVY COUNCILLOR, MAJOR.

MAJOR: Here, brother . . . I'm trailing around the place like Cain, restless and distracted. Shall I tell you something? They say the Russians are at war with the Turks: I'm going to Königsberg to hear more. I'll leave my wife and die in Turkey.

COUNCILLOR: These wild notions of yours are the last straw. Oh, heavens, must it blow from all directions at once? Read this letter from Professor M———r.

MAJOR: I can't read any more: I've wept myself well-nigh blind.

COUNCILLOR: Then I shall read it to you: you will see you are not the only father with cause to complain. "Your son was taken into custody some time ago as a surety; as he confessed to me with tears the day before yesterday, he has given up all hope of pardon by Your Excellency, having written five letters without response. I entreated him to calm himself until I had undertaken to mediate in this matter. He promised me this, but in spite of his promise escaped secretly from prison that very night. The creditors wished to send out summonses and publish his name in all the newspapers, but I prevented them and guaranteed the sum involved, for I am convinced that Your Excellency will not suffer this disgrace to your family. For the rest I have the honor, in expectation of your decision, to offer my most perfect etc., etc."

MAJOR: Write back and tell them to hang him.

COUNCILLOR: And the family . . . ?

MAJOR: Ridiculous! There is no family, we have no family. Fiddlesticks! The Russians are my family; I'll join the Greeks.

COUNCILLOR: And still no trace of your daughter?

MAJOR: What's that?

COUNCILLOR: Haven't you any news at all of your daughter?

MAJOR: Leave me alone.

COUNCILLOR: You can't be serious, surely, when you say you're going to Königsberg?

MAJOR: When is the mail coach from Königsberg to Warsaw likely to depart?

COUNCILLOR: I shan't let you go: there's no point in it, after all. Do you think sensible people will be taken in by your mad ideas? I declare you confined to quarters forthwith. Serious measures have to be taken with people like you, otherwise their grief turns to madness.

MAJOR (*weeps*): A whole year, brother, and no one knows whither she is fled or sped.

COUNCILLOR: Perhaps she is dead . . .

MAJOR: Perhaps? Dead for sure . . . could I only have the comfort of burying her, but she must have killed herself since no one can give me news of her. A bullet through my heart, Berg, or a Turkish saber—that were a victory indeed!

COUNCILLOR: It's just as likely that she met Läuffer somewhere and has fled the country with him. Yesterday Count Vermouth paid me a visit and said he had gone into a schoolhouse that same evening and the schoolmaster would not let him into the bedroom: he still suspects the tutor was hidden in there and perhaps your daughter with him.

MAJOR: Where's this schoolmaster of yours? Where's the village? And that scoundrel of a Count didn't force his way into the bedroom? Come on, where's the Count?

COUNCILLOR: He'll be staying at the Pike as usual.

MAJOR: Oh, if I could only find her, if I could only hope to see her once again. Damn it, old as I am and crazed with care, damn it all, I'd still summon up one more laugh, laugh out loud for the last time, lay my head in her dishonored lap,

lift up my voice once more in lamentation and then . . .
Adieu, Berg! That were a death for me! That's what I'd
call passing away gently and peacefully in the Lord! Come
along, brother: your son has just turned rogue. A trifle—
there are rogues at every court. But my daughter's a
common whore, that's what I call the joys of fatherhood.
Perhaps she has the three lilies branded on her back
already. Three cheers for private tutors—and may the
Devil take them!

SCENE TWO

A hovel in the woods. GUSTCHEN *in a coarse
smock;* MARTHA, *a blind old woman.*

GUSTCHEN: Martha dear, stay at home and mind the child.
It's the first time for a whole year I'm leaving you alone:
you can let me walk abroad by myself for once. You have
provisions for today and tomorrow, so you need not stand
and beg by the roadside today.

MARTHA: But where are you off to, Grete, for heaven's sake?
When you're so sick and weak. Listen to me: I have had
children myself, and without the pains you suffered, God
be thanked, but once I tried to go out on the second day
after the birth, but never again! I almost gave up the
ghost: in truth, I can tell you how the dead feel. Take a
lesson from me: if you have business in the next village I
can find my way there, blind as I am. You must stay at
home and get your strength back: I'll see to everything for
you, whatever it may be.

GUSTCHEN: Let me be, mother, I'm as strong as a young
she-bear. And look to my child.

MARTHA: But how shall I look to it, holy Mother of God,
when I'm blind? If it wants to suck, shall I put it to my
blackened, shrivelled tits? And you haven't the strength
to take it with you. Stay at home, dear Gretel, stay at
home!

GUSTCHEN: I may not, dear mother, my conscience drives me
from this place. I have a father who loves me more than

his life and soul. I dreamed last night I saw him with blood in his eyes, tearing his white hair. He will think I'm dead. I must go to the village and ask someone to give him news of me.

MARTHA: But, dear God, who is driving you away from here? If you should come to grief on the way? You cannot go . . .

GUSTCHEN: I must . . . my father stood swaying on his feet; suddenly he flung himself to the ground and lay there dead. He will kill himself if he has no news of me.

MARTHA: Don't you know that dreams go by opposites?

GUSTCHEN: Not with me. Let me go; God will be with me.

SCENE THREE

The schoolhouse. WENZESLAUS *and* LÄUFFER *sitting at a table. The* MAJOR, *the* COUNCILLOR, *and* COUNT VERMOUTH *enter with servants.*

WENZESLAUS (*drops his glasses*): Who's there?

MAJOR (*with drawn pistol*): A pox on you! There's the villain of the piece! (*Fires and hits* LÄUFFER *in the arm;* LÄUFFER *falls off his chair.*)

COUNCILLOR (*who has tried in vain to restrain the* MAJOR): Brother . . . (*Thrusts him angrily aside.*) On your own head be it, lunatic!

MAJOR: What? Is he dead? (*Strikes his forehead.*) What have I done? Is he past giving me news of my daughter?

WENZESLAUS: Gentlemen! Is the Last Judgment at hand, or what? What's all this? (*Tugs at the bellrope.*) I'll teach you to assault an honest man in his own home!

LÄUFFER: I beseech you not to ring the bell! It's the Major. I deserve this on account of his daughter.

COUNCILLOR: Isn't there a surgeon in the village, honest schoolmaster? He's only wounded in the arm; I'll have him treated.

WENZESLAUS: What do you mean, treated? Highwaymen! Do you riddle people with bullets just because you can afford to have them treated? He's my assistant; he's been exactly a year in my house, a quiet, peaceful, hardworking fellow

who never said a word out of season, and you come along
and shoot my assistant in my own home. You'll pay for this
or else I'll not die happy!

COUNCILLOR (*trying to bandage* LÄUFFER'*s arm*): What's the
good of all this talk, my dear fellow? We're sorry enough
for what's happened—but the man may bleed to death
from his wound. Just fetch us a surgeon.

WENZESLAUS: What? If you are going to inflict wounds, then
you may heal them, too. Highwaymen! Still, I may as well
fetch neighbor Schöpsen. (*Exit.*)

MAJOR (*to* LÄUFFER): Where's my daughter?

LÄUFFER: I don't know.

MAJOR: You don't know? (*Pulls out another pistol.*)

COUNCILLOR (*snatches the pistol from him and fires it out of
the window*): Must we chain you up, you . . .

LÄUFFER: I have not seen her since I ran away from your
house. I swear it to God, before whose judgment seat I soon
may stand.

MAJOR: So she did not run away with you?

LÄUFFER: No.

MAJOR: Well, then . . . another charge of powder shot off in
vain! I wish it had gone through your head, you scurvy
dog, since there's not a word of sense to be got out of you!
Let him lie there and come with me to the ends of the earth.
I must have my daughter again, and if not in this life, then
in another world, and neither my brilliant brother nor my
brilliant wife shall stop me, forsooth. (*Rushes off.*)

COUNCILLOR: I dare not let him out of my sight. (*Throws
LÄUFFER a purse.*) Have yourself treated with this, and
bear in mind that you have inflicted a graver injury on my
brother than he on you. There's a banker's draft in there:
take care of it and make what use of it you can. (*All go off;*
WENZESLAUS *returns with the barber* SCHÖPSEN *and a
number of farmhands.*)

WENZESLAUS: What's happened to that brood of vipers?
Speak!

LÄUFFER: Calm down, I beg you. I have got much less than my
deeds deserved. Master Schöpsen, is my wound dangerous?

(SCHÖPSEN *examines him.*)

WENZESLAUS: What's happened, then? Where are they? I'll
not put up with this, no, I won't, even if it costs me my
school and my employment, my hair and my beard! I'll
beat them to a pulp, the dogs! Just imagine, neighbor, who
ever heard of such a thing—*in jure naturae*, and *in jure
civili, in jure canonico* and *in jure gentium*, or whatever
else you please, whoever heard of an honest man invaded
in his own home and in a school, to boot! A hallowed
place!—Dangerous, eh? Have you probed the wound? Is
it serious?

SCHÖPSEN: A good deal might be said on that score . . . but,
well, we'll see . . . anyway, we'll see in the long run.

WENZESLAUS: Yes, sir, heh! heh! heh! *In fine videbitur
cuius toni*, that's to say, when he's dead or when he's quite
recovered, then you'll tell us whether the wound was
dangerous or not. But that's not medical parlance, I beg
your pardon. A good physician must know his stuff beforehand, otherwise I'll tell him to his face that he has only
half studied his pathology or his surgery and has gone to
the brothel more often than the lecture room. For *in
amore omnia insunt vitia*, and when I clap eyes on a dunce,
no matter what faculty he belongs to, I always say, he's
been a ladykiller, a whoremonger. And no one can tell me
different.

SCHÖPSEN (*after examining the wound again*): Yes, the wound
is so-so, as you might say . . . we shall see, we shall see.

LÄUFFER: Here, schoolmaster! The Major's brother left me a
purse heavy with ducats, and there's a banker's draft in it
as well. We're set up for years to come.

WENZESLAUS (*picks up the purse*): Well, that's something.
But trespass is trespass and sacrilege sacrilege, all the same.
I'll write him a letter, that Major, that he'll not care to
display in his parlor window.

SCHÖPSEN (*has forgotten himself meanwhile and has been
staring hard at the purse; he now busies himself once more
with the wound*): It will heal in the end, never fear, but it
will be difficult, difficult, I hope . . .

WENZESLAUS: And I hope not, neighbor Schöpsen, I fear it, I
fear it, but I'll tell you something for a start—if you cure

the wound slowly, then you'll be paid slowly, but if you put him back on his feet in two days, then you'll be paid without delay. You can make your arrangements accordingly.

SCHÖPSEN: We shall see . . .

SCENE FOUR

GUSTCHEN *lies beside a pond surrounded by bushes.*

GUSTCHEN: Am I to die here, then? Father! Father! Do not blame me that you heard no news of me. I have spent the last reserves of my strength—now they are finally used up! I see him constantly before my eyes! He's dead, yes, dead —and from grieving over me. His ghost appeared to me last night, to tell me of it, to call me to account. I am coming, I'm coming! (*Drags herself to her feet and leaps into the pond.*)

(MAJOR *in the distance, the* PRIVY COUNCILLOR *and* COUNT VERMOUTH *following him.*)

MAJOR: Hey! Ho! Something fell into the pond. 'Twas a female, and even if it wasn't my daughter it's an unhappy female! After her, Berg! This is the path to Gustchen or to hell!

COUNCILLOR (*enters*): Heavens! What shall we do?

COUNT: I can't swim.

COUNCILLOR: Round the other side! I do believe he's got hold of the girl . . . There, there in the bushes yonder! Can't you see? Now he's drifting down the pond with her. After them!

SCENE FIVE

The other side of the pond.

MAJOR: (*shouting offstage*): Help! It's my daughter! Damn and blast it all! Count! Reach me that pole, can't you!

Blast you! (MAJOR *carries* GUSTCHEN *onto the stage. The* PRIVY COUNCILLOR *and the* COUNT *follow him.*)

MAJOR: There! (*Puts her down; the* COUNCILLOR *and the* COUNT *try to revive her.*) Confounded child! Is that what I had you brought up for? (*Kneels down beside her.*) Gustel! What's the matter? Have you swallowed some water? Are you still my Gustel? God-forsaken baggage! If only you'd said one word to me, I'd have bought the fellow a patent of nobility, and then you could have cuddled to your heart's content. God forbid! Help her, can't you! She's in a swoon. (*Jumps up, wrings his hands, paces up and down.*) If only I knew where we could find the confounded village surgeon. Hasn't she come round?

GUSTCHEN (*in a feeble voice*): Father!

MAJOR: What do you want?

GUSTCHEN: Pardon!

MAJOR (*goes over to her*): May the devil pardon you, naughty child! No! (*Kneels down beside her.*) Don't swoon, my Gustel, my Gustel! I pardon you, everything's forgiven and forgotten. God knows, I pardon you. It's you should pardon me! But now it's too late: I've put a bullet through the scoundrel's head.

COUNCILLOR: I think we should get her away from here.

MAJOR: Leave her alone! What's she to you? She's not your daughter, you know. Mind your own flesh and blood at home! (*He takes* GUSTCHEN *up in his arms.*) There, girl— I really ought to put you back in the pond (*swings her toward the pond*)—but we'll not go swimming, I don't think, until we've learned to swim. (*Clutches her to his heart.*) Oh, my only dearest treasure! To think I can carry you in my arms once more, you God-forsaken baggage! (*Carries her off.*)

SCENE SIX

Leipzig. FRITZ VON BERG, PÄTUS.

FRITZ: There's only one fault I have to find with you, Pätus. I've been meaning to tell you for ages. Just take a good look at yourself: what has been the cause of all your misfortunes? I wouldn't chide a fellow for falling in love. It's our time of life: we're on the high seas, the wind drives us on, but reason must always be at the helm, otherwise we run upon the nearest reef and are dashed to pieces. Fräulein Hamster was a flirt who did exactly as she liked with you; she robbed you of your last coat, of your good name and the good name of your friends as well: I would have thought you had learned your lesson from all this. Fräulein Rehaar is an innocent young lamb who has never been seduced. If you bring all your batteries to bear upon a heart that will not —cannot—defend itself, in order to—what shall I say?— to destroy it, to reduce it to ashes, then that's wrong, Brother Pätus, that's wrong. Don't take it amiss, but in that case we could not remain friends. A man who goes as far with a woman as he possibly can is either a nincompoop or a villain: a nincompoop if he cannot hold himself in check and loses sight of the respect he owes to innocence and virtue, or a villain if he will not hold himself in check and, like the Devil in the Garden of Eden, finds his only pleasure in ruining a woman.

PÄTUS: No need to preach, brother! You are right; I regret it, but I swear to you, I can take my oath on it, I haven't laid a finger on the girl.

FRITZ: But you climbed in at her window nevertheless, and the neighbors saw you. Do you think their tongues will be as chaste as your hand may have been? I know you: bold as you may seem, you are shy with women, and that is why I am fond of you. But even if it were only a matter of robbing the girl of her good name, a musician's daughter at that, a girl endowed by nature and not by fortune—to rob her of her only dowry, her good name—you have wrecked her prospects, Pätus . . .

(*Enter* REHAAR, *a lute under his arm.*)

REHAAR: Your humble servant, your humble servant, Herr von Berg, I wish you a very good morning. How have you slept, and how is our little concerto? (*Sits down and begins to tune the instrument.*) Have you played it through? (*Tuning.*) I had such a dreadful fright last night, but I'll get my own back on the fellow—you know him well, it's one of your fellow countrymen. Twing, twing! Confounded E-string! 'Pon my soul, it just won't sound right; I'll bring you another this afternoon.

FRITZ (*sits down with his lute*): I haven't looked at the concerto yet.

REHAAR: Tut, tut, lazy Herr von Bergikins! Not looked at it? Twing! I'll bring you another this afternoon. (*Puts down the lute and takes a pinch of snuff.*) They say the Turks have crossed the Danube and have given the Russians a fine thrashing and driven them back to . . . what's the name of the place again? To Ochakov, I think, or something like that. But I'll tell you one thing: if Rehaar had been among them, what d'you think, he'd have run a lot further still! Ha, ha, ha! (*Picks up the lute again.*) I tell you, Herr von Berg, nothing pleases me more than when I read in the newspaper that an army has taken to its heels. Stout fellows, the Russians, to run away! Rehaar would have run, too, and so would any sensible man; what's the good of standing there to be killed, ha, ha, ha!

FRITZ: This is the first position of fingering, isn't it?

REHAAR: Quite right: second finger a little more across here, your little finger lifted, so . . . A nice rounded trill, rounded, Herr von Bergikins! My late father always used to say, a musician needs no pluck, and a stout-hearted musician is a knave. As long as he can play his little concerto and sound his march well enough . . . That's what I said to the Duke of Courland when I went to Saint Petersburg for the first time in the suite of Prince Czartorinsky and had to perform before him. I can't help laughing still. When I came into the *salon* and made to bow very, very low, I didn't notice the floor was of mirror glass, and the walls as well, and I fell down like a chunk of wood and knocked a mighty hole in my head. Then the courtiers came along and meant to tease me. Don't put up with it, Rehaar, said the Duke, you wear a sword, don't you; don't put up with it. Well, yes, Your Grace, said I, but my sword hasn't been out of its sheath since the year 'thirty, and a plucky musician who draws his sword is a knave and fit for nothing on any instrument . . . No, no, the third chord it was, like this . . . Pure, pure, a nice full trill, and don't move your thumb down there, that's it . . .

PÄTUS (*who has been standing to one side, comes forward and offers* REHAAR *his hand*): Your servant, Herr Rehaar. How goes it?

REHAAR (*gets up, holding the lute*): Humble serv . . . How should it go, Herr Pätus? *Toujours content, jamais d'argent:* that's old Rehaar's motto, you know, and all the students know it—but they still don't give me anything. Herr Pätus still owes me money from the last serenade, but he never thinks of it . . .

PÄTUS: You shall have it, my dear Rehaar; I expect my allowance without fail next week.

REHAAR: Yes, you have waited a long time, Herr Pätus, and your allowance hasn't come. What can one do, one must have patience, I always say. No one commands my respect more than a student: a student's a nobody, it's true, but he may well turn into a somebody. (*Puts the lute on the table and takes a pinch of snuff.*) But what have you done to me, Herr Pätus? Was that right, was that a decent way to go on? Climbing in at my window last night, into my daughter's bedroom.

PÄTUS: What's all this, old man? Me? . . .

REHAAR (*drops his snuffbox*): I'll "old man" you! And I'll see it's made known in the proper quarter, sir, you may be sure of that. My daughter's good name is precious to me, and she's a respectable girl, Devil take me! And if only I'd noticed last night or if I'd woken up, I'd have hustled you out of that window head over heels . . . Is it decent, is it honest? Damn it all, if I'm a student, then I have to behave like a student, not like a lout! The neighbors told me today: I thought I'd have a fit. I've packed the girl off on the coach to her aunt in Courland; yes, to Courland, sir, for her good name is ruined here—and who's to pay the fare, eh? Truly, I haven't touched a lute all day, and at least fifteen E-strings have snapped. Yes, sir, I'm still all of a tremble, and I've a bone to pick with you, Herr Pätus. It shan't rest here; I'll teach you louts to seduce honest people's children!

Pätus: Don't insult me, sir, or else . . .

Rehaar: Just look at that, Herr von Berg, just look at that—if I had the pluck I'd challenge him to draw this instant! Look —there he stands—and laughs in my face, what's more. Are we among Turks and heathens, then, that a father's not safe with his daughter? Herr Pätus, you'll not get away with this, I tell you, if it has to go to the Elector himself. Into the army with such dissolute dogs! Follow the drum, that's the thing for them! Louts you are, not students!

Pätus (*slaps* Rehaar's *face*): Don't you dare insult me; I've told you half a dozen times!

Rehaar (*jumps up, holding his handkerchief to his face*): So! Just wait—if only I could keep the weal on my cheek until I appear before the Rector—if only I could keep it for a week until I travel to Dresden and show it to the Elector. Just wait, I'll pay you back, just wait! Is this to be allowed? (*Weeps.*) To strike a lutist? Because he won't give you his daughter to play your little lute upon? Just wait, I'll tell His Majesty the Elector that you struck me in the face. They shall chop your hand off! Lout! (*Runs off;* Pätus *makes to follow him, but* Fritz *holds him back.*)

Fritz: Pätus! You have behaved badly. He was an offended father; you should have spared his feelings.

Pätus: Why did the knave have to insult me?

Fritz: Insulting behavior deserves insult. There was no other way he could redeem his daughter's good name, but there might be others . . .

Pätus: What? What others?

Fritz: You've dishonored her, you've dishonored her father. Only a scoundrel would take advantage of women—and musicians, who are less than women!

Pätus: A scoundrel?

Fritz: You must offer him a public apology.

Pätus: With my cane!

Fritz: Then I shall answer you in his name.

Pätus (*shouting*): What do you want of me?

Fritz: Satisfaction for Rehaar.

Pätus: Surely you don't mean to force me, you simpleton, to . . .

FRITZ: Yes, I'll force you not to be a rogue.

PÄTUS: Rogue yourself! You'll fight me for that!

FRITZ: With all my heart—if you don't give Rehaar satisfaction.

PÄTUS: Never!

FRITZ: We shall see.

ACT FIVE

SCENE ONE

The schoolhouse. LÄUFFER, MARTHA *with a child
in her arms.*

MARTHA: For heaven's sake! Help a poor blind old woman and a blameless child that's lost its mother.

LÄUFFER (*gives her a coin*): How have you come this far, if you cannot see?

MARTHA: With toil enough. The mother of this child used to be my guide. She left home one day, only two days after her confinement, she left at noon and meant to return by evening; she has still not come back. May God grant her everlasting joy and glory!

LÄUFFER: Why do you make that wish?

MARTHA: Because she's dead, the good woman; otherwise she'd not have broken her word. A laborer from up the hill met me, he saw her throw herself into the pond. An old man ran after her and threw himself in, too. That must have been her father.

LÄUFFER: Oh, heavens! How I tremble—is that her child?

MARTHA: It is. Just see how pot-bellied it is, fed on nothing but cabbage and turnips. What else should I do, wretched woman that I am; I could not suckle it, and when all my provisions were gone, I took the child upon my shoulder like Hagar and set out to seek God's mercy.

LÄUFFER: Put it in my arms. Oh, my heart! That I can press it to my heart! Awful enigma—solved before my eyes! (*Takes the child in his arms and goes to the mirror.*) What's this? Are these not my features? (*Falls in a faint; the child begins to scream.*)

MARTHA: Have you fallen down? (*Lifts the child off the ground.*) Sweetheart, my darling sweetheart! (*The child is quiet.*) Hark! What have you done? He doesn't answer. I must call for help; I do believe he's done himself an injury. (*Exit.*)

SCENE TWO

A wood on the outskirts of Leipzig. FRITZ VON BERG *and* PÄTUS *standing with drawn swords;* REHAAR.

FRITZ: Come on, then!

PÄTUS: Why don't you start?

FRITZ: You start!

PÄTUS (*throws down his sword*): I cannot fight with you.

FRITZ: Why not? Pick up your sword. If I have insulted you then I must give you satisfaction.

PÄTUS: You may insult me as you please, I seek no satisfaction from you.

FRITZ: You insult me!

PÄTUS (*runs up to him and throws his arms round him*): My dearest Berg! Do not take it as an insult when I tell you that you are incapable of insulting me. I know your heart and the very thought of it makes me the sorriest poltroon on earth. Let us remain good friends. I'll duel with the Devil himself, but not with you!

FRITZ: Then give Rehaar satisfaction, otherwise I'll not leave this spot.

PÄTUS: That I'll do with all my heart, if he wants it.

FRITZ: He's a member of the university, as you are; you struck him in the face. Come on, Rehaar—draw!

REHAAR (*draws his sword*): Yes, but he mustn't pick up his sword.

FRITZ: You're out of your mind! Do you mean to draw your sword on a man who can't defend himself?

REHAAR: Oh, let those who have the pluck draw on armed opponents! A musician needs no pluck, and, Herr Pätus, you shall give me satisfaction. (*Lunges at him;* PÄTUS *draws back.*) Give me satisfaction. (*Stabs* PÄTUS *in the arm;* FRITZ *strikes up* REHAAR's *sword.*)

FRITZ: Now I can see you merit a box on the ears. Fie!

REHAAR: What am I supposed to do, then, if I'm not a man of pluck?

FRITZ: Take your box on the ears and keep your mouth shut.

PÄTUS: Quiet, Berg, it's only a scratch. Herr Rehaar, I beg your pardon. I ought not to have struck you since I knew you were not in a position to demand satisfaction; still less should I have given you occasion to insult me. I admit that this revenge is still too slight for the injuries I have inflicted on your family. I'll see that I make them good in some more fitting fashion, if fortune favors my good intentions. I shall follow your daughter; I wish to marry her. There will be some employment or other for me in my own country, and even if my father were not persuaded to a change of heart during his lifetime, I may still depend upon a legacy of fifteen thousand gulden. (*Embraces* REHAAR.) Will you grant me you daughter's hand?

REHAAR: Well, now! I've nothing against the match, provided you ask for her hand honestly and in due form, and provided you're in a position to keep her. Ha, ha, ha! I've always said, students are easy to get on with. They are decent at heart, but officers—they get a girl with child and no one gives a damn: that's because they are all plucky fellows and have to stand there and get killed. For your plucky man is capable of all sorts of vices.

FRITZ: You're a student yourself, after all. Come along, it's ages since we brewed a punch together. We'll drink to the health of your daughter.

REHAAR: Yes, and we'll have your little lute concerto along with it, Herr von Bergikins. I've skipped three lessons on end, and because I'm a decent chap, I'll spend three hours on end in your little room, and we'll play our little lutes until it's dark.

PÄTUS: And I'll accompany you on the fiddle.

SCENE THREE

The schoolhouse. LÄUFFER *lying in bed,* WENZESLAUS.

WENZESLAUS: For God's sake! What's the matter now, that you have me fetched from work? Are you feeling faint again? I do believe the old woman was a witch. Since she was here you haven't had a single hour's good health.

LÄUFFER: I'm not long for this world.

WENZESLAUS: Shall I fetch neighbor Schöpsen?

LÄUFFER: No.

WENZESLAUS: Have you something on your conscience? Tell me, reveal it to me frankly. You keep looking round so nervously, it's enough to send shivers down my spine: *frigidus per ossa.* Tell me, what's the trouble? As if he'd murdered someone! What are you pulling such faces for? So help me God, I must fetch Schöpsen after all . . .

LÄUFFER: Stop. I don't know whether I've done right. I've castrated myself . . .

WENZESLAUS: Wha—! Castr—! My most heartfelt congratulations! Splendid, young man! A second Origen! Allow me to embrace you, most cherished chosen instrument! I cannot conceal from you that I am barely—barely able to resist the heroic resolve to follow your example. How right you are, my esteemed friend! This is the path by which you may become a luminary of the Church, a star of the first order, a Father of the Church, even! I congratulate you, I hail with a *Jubilate* and an *Evoë*, my spiritual son . . . Were I not already beyond the years when the Devil lays his most subtle snares for our prime and finest powers, indeed I would not for one moment pause to think . . .

LÄUFFER: All the same, schoolmaster, I rue it.

WENZESLAUS: What, you rue it? Far from it, esteemed confrater! Surely you will not overshadow such a noble deed with remorse and sully it by sinful tears? I see them welling on your lids already. Swallow them and sing aloud with joy: I am delivered from nothingness, give me wings, wings, wings! I hope you'll not be like Lot's wife and turn to look back on Sodom when you have already attained the peace and calm of Zoar? No, dear colleague: I must tell you, however, you are not the only one to have this idea. Even among the Jews in their spiritual blindness there was a sect, to which I'd gladly have declared my public allegiance, had I not feared to affront my neighbors and the poor lambs in my school . . . in any case, they had, it's true, some foolish dross of superstition in their faith that I'd no truck with. For instance, that they might not even pass their water on the Sabbath, which is against all the rules of a sensible diet, and there I rather take the part of our late blessed Doctor Luther: what goes up is for God, what goes down, Devil, is yours . . . Now, where was I?

LÄUFFER: I fear my motives were of another sort . . . remorse, despair . . .

WENZESLAUS: Yes, now I have it! The Essenes, I say, never took wives to themselves; it was one of their principles, and they lived to a ripe old age, as you may read in Josephus. How they made a start in thus mortifying the flesh, whether they did it like me, living sober, temperate lives and cheerfully smoking their tobacco, or whether they chose your way . . . so much is certain, *in amore, in amore insunt omnia vitia*, and a youth who weathers this headland—hail to him, all hail, I'll shower him with laurels: *lauro tempora cingam et sublimi fronte sidera pulsabit.*

LÄUFFER: I fear I shall die of the incision.

WENZESLAUS: Not a bit of it; God forbid! I'll go straight to neighbor Schöpsen. He won't ever have encountered such a case, it's true, but he healed your arm, which after all was a wound that was not conducive to your spiritual well-being, so God will certainly vouchsafe him a cure when it's in the interests of your everlasting salvation. (*Exit.*)

LÄUFFER: His exultation wounds me more painfully than my knife did. Oh, innocence, what a pearl thou art! Since I lost thee I have advanced step by step ever deeper into passion and ended in despair. Oh, that this last step might not lead me unto death: perhaps I might begin to live again and be reborn a second Wenzeslaus.

SCENE FOUR

Leipzig. FRITZ VON BERG *and* REHAAR *meet in the street.*

REHAAR: Herr von Bergikins! A little note enclosed in a letter to me. Herr von Seiffenblase has written to me: he learned to play the lute with me, as you did. He asks me to give this note to a certain Herr von Berg in Leipzig, supposing he's still there. Oh, how I've run!

FRITZ: Where is he staying now, Seiffenblase?

REHAAR: Should give it to Herr von Berg, he writes, if you know the worthy man. Oh, how I've run! He's in Königsberg, Herr von Seiffenblase. What do you think: my daughter is there too and lodges just across the street from him. Little Katherine writes that she cannot speak too highly of the civility he shows her—all for my sake. He took lessons from me for seven months.

FRITZ (*takes out his watch*): My dear Herr Rehaar, I have to go to a lecture. Say nothing of this to Pätus, I beg you. (*Exit.*)

REHAAR (*calls after him*): See you this afternoon . . . your little concerto . . .

SCENE FIVE

Königsberg in Prussia. PRIVY COUNCILLOR, GUSTCHEN, MAJOR, *all standing by the window.*

COUNCILLOR: Is it him?

GUSTCHEN: Yes, that's him.

COUNCILLOR: I can see the aunt must be an abandoned creature, or else she's conceived a hatred for her niece and is deliberately trying to ruin her.

GUSTCHEN: But, uncle, she cannot ban him from the house.

COUNCILLOR: On the evidence I gave her? Who would take it amiss if she were to say to him: Herr von Seiffenblase, you have stated publicly in a coffeehouse that you meant to make my niece your mistress. Find yourself other acquaintances in the town, you are out of place in my house.

My niece is from abroad and entrusted to my care; she has no other support. If she were seduced the entire blame would fall on me. God and men alike would condemn me.

MAJOR: Be quiet, brother! He's coming out with a wretched, hangdog look. Ho, ho, ho! May you rot! How pale he is.

COUNCILLOR: I'll go across this minute and see what has happened.

SCENE SIX

Leipzig. PÄTUS *at a table, writing.*
BERG *enters with a letter in his hand.*
PÄTUS *looks up, then goes on writing.*

FRITZ: Pätus, are you busy?

PÄTUS: Just a moment. (FRITZ *paces up and down.*) Now! (PATUS *puts away his pen and paper.*)

FRITZ: I have had a letter—and I haven't the heart to open it.

PÄTUS: Where's it from? Is it your father's hand?

FRITZ: No, from Seiffenblase . . . but my hand shakes so whenever I try to open it. You open it, brother, and read it to me. (*Throws himself into an armchair.*)

PÄTUS (*reads*): "The recollection of so many pleasurable hours which I recall having enjoyed in your company obliges me to write to you and remind you of those pleasurable hours . . ." The boy's spelling is crazy.

FRITZ: Just read it.

PÄTUS: "And because I felt obliged to give you news of my arrival and of the latest events here, I have to inform you concerning your most esteemed family, which unfortunately has suffered many misfortunes this past year, and on account of the friendship which I enjoyed in the home of your parents, I see myself obliged, because I know that you are at odds with your father and he will not have written to you for a long time, so that you will not know of the mishap with the private tutor, who has been thrown out of your uncle's house because he raped your cousin, which she took so much to heart that she jumped into a pond, by which sad event your family suffered the most violent shock . . ." Berg, what's the matter? (*Pours lavender water over him.*) What now, Berg? Speak, are you in pain? If only . . . that damned letter . . . It's bound to be a pure invention . . . Berg! Berg!

FRITZ: Leave me alone . . . it will pass.

PÄTUS: Shall I fetch someone to bleed you?

FRITZ: Oh, fie! Don't be such a fusspot.

PÄTUS: Yes, I'll . . . I'll tear up the rascally malicious thing this moment! (*Tears letter.*)

FRITZ: Raped . . . drowned! (*Strikes his forehead with his clenched fist.*) My fault! (*Stands up.*) All my fault and none but mine . . .

PÄTUS: Don't be an ass! Do you blame yourself because she allowed herself to be seduced by the tutor?

FRITZ: Pätus, I swore to her that I'd return, I swore it. Three years have passed and I didn't come. I left Halle, my father has had no news of me. My father has given me up for lost, she heard of it . . . grief . . . you know her tendency to melancholy . . . her mother's strictness into the bargain, solitude in the country, love deceived . . . Can't you see, Pätus, can't you see that? I'm a villain, I'm to blame for her death. (*Throws himself into a chair and covers his face with his hands.*)

PÄTUS: Imagination! It isn't true, it didn't happen like that. (*Stamps his foot.*) Poppycock and fiddlesticks, how can you be so stupid as to believe it all: that rascal, that knave, that idle rogue Seiffenblase is out to play a trick on you! Just let me clap eyes on him! It isn't true that she's dead, and if she is dead, then she didn't kill herself . . .

FRITZ: But he can't have made it all up out of thin air. Killed ·herself! (*Jumps up.*) Oh, this is terrible!

PÄTUS (*stamps his foot again*): No, she hasn't killed herself. Seiffenblase's lying. We must have more proof. You know you once told him when you were drunk that you were in love with your cousin. You see, the wicked scum has picked that up—but let me tell you something: d'you know what you're going to do? Send him about his business; give him

the bird; send him away with a flea in his ear! Write to
him: I am most humbly grateful, sir, for your news—be
pleased to lick my arse! That's the best advice. Write back
to him: You are a villain, sir! That's the most sensible
thing you can do in this affair!

FRITZ: I shall go home.

PÄTUS: Then I'll go with you. Berg, I'll not leave you by
yourself for a moment!

FRITZ: But how shall we pay for the journey? It's all very well
to say "go home." If I didn't fear a refusal I'd try Leichtfuss and Company, but I already owe them a hundred and
fifty ducats . . .

PÄTUS: We'll go and see them together. Wait a minute: we
have to pass the lottery office on the way. The mail from
Hamburg comes in today, I'll inquire on our way, just for
a laugh . . .

SCENE SEVEN

Königsberg. PRIVY COUNCILLOR *leads in*
FRÄULEIN REHAAR *by the hand;* GUSTCHEN, MAJOR.

COUNCILLOR: Here, Gustchen, I have brought you a playmate.
You are the same age and in the same situation. Shake
hands and be friends.

GUSTCHEN: That I have long been, dear Fräulein Rehaar!
I find it hard to say what feelings stirred in my breast when
I observed you from the window. But you were so taken up
with so many distractions, so beset by carriage calls and
serenades that I feared to call at an inopportune moment.

FRÄULEIN REHAAR: I would have forestalled you, Fräulein
von Berg, if I had had the heart. But to force my way into
such a distinguished household seemed to me untimely,
and I had to resist with all my might the impulse of my
heart that led me so often to your doorstep.

COUNCILLOR: Just think, Major: Seiffenblase replied to the
warning I gave Frau Dutzend and which she passed on to
him in my name, as I requested her, that he would find

ways to pay me back. He was well able to repudiate the whole story and drove up the next day with Minister Deichsel, so that the poor woman had not the heart to forbid his visits. Last night he gave instructions for two coaches to come to this street and for a third to go to the Brandenburg Gate, that was left open because of the firework display. Frau Dutzend heard of this yesterday morning. In the afternoon he tried by every means in his power to persuade the young lady that she should go with him to the Minister's reception, but Frau Dutzend had her suspicions and refused him outright. He drove up to the door but had to leave again. Having played his cards to no avail he meant to try again today. Frau Dutzend not only banned him from the house but gave him to understand at the same time that she had no alternative but to request the governor to place a guard upon her home. At this he breathed fire and fury, and threatened her with the Minister. In order to reassure Frau Dutzend beyond all doubt I have offered to take the young lady into our house. We'll take her with us to Insterburg for six months until Seiffenblase has forgotten her—or for as long as she's pleased to stay there . . .

MAJOR: I've had the horses put to. When we go to Heidelbrunn, young lady, I'll not allow you to leave us. You'll have to come along, or else my daughter will stay and keep you company in Insterburg.

COUNCILLOR: That would no doubt be best. The country doesn't suit Gustchen in any case, and I'll not be parted from Fräulein Rehaar.

MAJOR: A good thing your wife can't hear you . . . or are you thinking of your son?

COUNCILLOR: Don't make the poor child blush. You'll have seen enough of him in Leipzig, Fräulein Rehaar, the wicked lad. Gustchen, are you blushing as well? He doesn't deserve it.

GUSTCHEN: Since my father has forgiven me, should your son find a less indulgent heart in you?

COUNCILLOR: He has yet to jump into a pond.

MAJOR: If only we had traced the blind woman with the child that the schoolmaster wrote to me about: I shall have no peace of mind until we find her. Come along, I must get back to my farm today.

COUNCILLOR: Out of the question. You'll have to sleep in Insterburg tonight.

SCENE EIGHT

Leipzig. BERG's *room.* FRITZ VON BERG *sitting with his head in his hand.* PÄTUS *rushes in.*

PÄTUS: Triumph, Berg! What are you moping there for? God! God! (*Clutches his head and falls on his knees.*) Destiny! Destiny! Leichtfuss wouldn't make you an advance, would he? Let him get . . . I have money, I have everything! I've won 380 Friedrichs d'or at a stroke! (*Jumps up and shouts.*) Hi-diddle-dum! To Insterburg! Pack your things!

FRITZ: Have you gone mad?

PÄTUS (*pulls out a purse with gold and flings coins on the floor*): There's my madness. It's you that's the madman, with your doubts. Now help me pick all this up . . . down on your knees! And it's off to Insterburg, this very day! Hurrah! (*They pick up the coins.*) I'll make my father a present of eighty Friedrichs d'or—my last allowance was that much—and I'll say to him: Well, papa, how do you like me now? We can pay off all your debts and mine into the bargain, and then we'll travel like princes! Hurrah!

SCENE NINE

The schoolhouse. WENZESLAUS, LÄUFFER, *both dressed in black.*

WENZESLAUS: How did you like the sermon, colleague? Did you find it edifying?

LÄUFFER: Good, very good. (*Sighs.*)

WENZESLAUS (*removes his wig and puts on a nightcap*): That won't do. You must tell me which passage most particularly shed a blessing on your heart. Listen—sit down. I have something to say to you. In church I made an observation that weighed upon my mind. It seemed to me you were sitting there as wayward as a weathercock. To tell the truth, I was ashamed of you in front of the whole congregation; you almost put me quite out of countenance more than once. What, I thought, this young warrior who has gained a victory worthy of any knight and has all but survived the heat of the battle ... I must confess, you vexed me, *skandalon edidous hetaire*! I saw perfectly well what you had your eye on, perfectly well: your gaze was never off the center doorway, down toward the organ, there.

LÄUFFER: I must admit there was a painting hanging there that quite distracted me. The Evangelist Mark with a face that looked not one whit more human than the lion sitting beside him, and the angel with the Evangelist Matthew looking a good deal more like a winged serpent than an angel.

WENZESLAUS: It wasn't that, my friend! Don't imagine that it was. It wasn't that. Tell me now: we look at a picture and then we look away again, and that's that. Did you hear what I was saying? Are you in a position to quote a single word from my sermon? And in fact it was given entirely for your benefit, a piece of special pleading. Oh, oh, oh!

LÄUFFER: The idea particularly appealed to me that a great similarity prevails between our soul and its regeneration, on the one hand, and the cultivation of hemp and flax, on the other; just as the hemp in the threshing board has to be freed from its old husk by violent blows and beating, so must our spirit be prepared for heaven by all kinds of trials and tribulations and mortification of the senses.

WENZESLAUS: It was special pleading, my friend.

LÄUFFER: All the same I cannot conceal from you that your catalogue of devils expelled from heaven, and the history of the whole revolt there, and the fact that Lucifer believed himself to be the fairest ... The world of today has long ago outgrown such superstitions: why seek to dish them up again? No one in the entire rational world nowadays supposes there is a Devil ...

WENZESLAUS: And that's why the entire rational world will
go to the Devil! I have no wish to condemn, my dear Herr
Mandel, but there's no denying we live in spiritually
ruinous times: this is the ultimate age of iniquity. I don't
care to enlarge upon this: I can see you are a skeptic, and
one has to suffer such people. The time will come all right,
you are still young . . . but even supposing—*posito*, but
I'm not admitting it—supposing our dogmas were all
nothing but superstitions concerning ghosts, hell, devils
and so on—what's it to you, why does it irk you, so that
you fight against it, tooth and nail? Do no evil, do what is
right, and then you need not fear the devils, even though
there might be more of them than tiles on the roof, as our
blessed Luther used to say. And superstition . . . oh, hold
your peace, hold your peace, dear friends! Just consider on
mature reflection what benefit superstition has conferred
on us hitherto, and then come at me with your prosy
raillery, if you have the heart. I'd like to see you root out
superstition! To be sure, the true faith would perish as well,
and a barren field remain. But I know of someone who said,
let them both grow side by side, a time will come when the
crop will be separated from the weeds. Superstition—
deprive the mob of their superstitions, and they'll speculate
like you and break your head. Take away the peasant's
devil and he'll turn into a devil toward his landlord and
prove to him that devils do exist. But leaving that aside . . .
what was I saying? Oh, yes, tell me, who were you gazing
at throughout the entire sermon? Don't try to hide anything from me. It certainly wasn't me, unless you had an
absolutely deplorable squint.

LÄUFFER: The picture.

WENZESLAUS: It wasn't the picture. Down there, where the
girls sit who come to your classes. Dear friend, I hope
there's nothing of the old leaven left in your heart! Oh,
oh! He, who has tasted the powers of the world hereafter
. . . I pray you, you make my hair stand on end . . . the
one with the yellow hair so casually pushed under the red
bonnet, isn't it? And with the brown eyes that sparkle all
the time under her dark eyebrows as roguishly as stars

through rainclouds. The girl is dangerous, to be sure; I saw her only once from the pulpit, and after that I always had to shut my eyes tight when they lighted upon her, otherwise I'd have suffered the same fate as the wise men of the Areopagus, who forgot law and justice on account of a vile Phryne. But tell me, what's the point of indulging in wicked lusts when you lack the very means to gratify them? Do you mean to surrender yourself to the Devil for nothing? Is that the vow you swore to the Lord—I speak to you as your spiritual father—you, who might with so little effort triumph over every sensual impulse, soar beyond this earth and take flight to higher regions. (*Embraces* LÄUFFER.) Oh, my dear son, by these tears that I shed out of truly heartfelt concern for you, return not to the fleshpots of Egypt when you were so near unto Canaan! Make haste! Make haste! Save your immortal soul! You have nothing more on earth to hold you back. The world possesses nothing more with which it might reward your infidelity even. Not even a sensual joy, much less serenity of soul. I will go and leave you to make your choice. (*Exit;* LÄUFFER *remains, plunged in thought.*)

SCENE TEN

LISE *enters, a hymnbook in her hand, without*
LÄUFFER's *noticing her. She watches him for a*
long time in silence. He jumps to his feet and
makes to kneel down, catches sight of LISE *and*
looks at her for a moment in confusion.

LÄUFFER (*approaches her*): You have filched a soul from heaven. (*Catches hold of her hand.*) What brings you here, Lise?

LISE: I came, Herr Mandel . . . I came, because you said there would be no class tomorrow . . . because you . . . I came . . . because you said . . . I came to ask . . . if there will be a class tomorrow.

LÄUFFER: Oh! Behold these cheeks, ye angels! How they burn with chaste fire—and then condemn me, if you can . . . Lise, why is your hand trembling? Why are your lips so pale and your cheeks so red? What do you want?

LISE: Will there be a class tomorrow?

LÄUFFER: Sit down beside me . . . Put away your hymnbook . . . Who pins up your hair when you go to church? (*Seats her on a chair next to his.*)

LISE (*about to get up*): Excuse me: my bonnet is not properly pinned on; there was such a dreadful wind when I set off for church.

LÄUFFER (*takes both her hands in his*): Oh, you are . . . How old are you, Lise? Have you never . . . What did I mean to ask you? . . . Have you never had suitors?

LISE (*cheerfully*): Oh, yes, one, just last week. And Grete, the shepherd's daughter, was so jealous of me and kept saying: I don't know why he bothers with that simpleton. And then I had an officer—not more than three months since.

LÄUFFER: An officer?

LISE: Yes, that's right. And a real swell, too, I can tell you; he had three stripes on his sleeve, but I was still too young, and my father didn't want him to have me on account of his soldier's ways and moving about, and all that.

LÄUFFER: Would you . . . Oh, I don't know what I'm saying . . . Would you . . . Wretch that I am!

LISE: Oh, yes, with all my heart.

LÄUFFER: My charmer! (*Tries to kiss her hand.*) You don't even know what I was going to ask you.

LISE (*pulls her hand away*): Oh, don't, my hand's too grubby! Oh, fie, what are you doing? I'd love to have a clerical gentleman, you see. Ever since I was a little girl I've been fond of learned gentlemen: they're always so nice and polite, not so crash-bang like the soldiers, although in a way I'm fond of them as well, I don't deny, on account of their colored coats. I'm sure if clerical gentlemen wore such brightly colored coats I'd simply die!

LÄUFFER: Let me seal your wanton mouth with my lips! (*Kisses her.*) Oh, Lise, if only you knew how unhappy I am.

LISE: Oh, fie, sir! What are you doing?

LÄUFFER: Once more, and then never again! (*Kisses her.* WENZESLAUS *enters.*)

WENZESLAUS: What's this? *Proh deum atque hominum fidem?* How now, false, false, false prophet! Ravening wolf in sheep's clothing! Is this the solicitude you owe your flock? Yourself seducing the very innocence you should shield from seduction? For it must needs be that offenses come; but woe to that man by whom the offense cometh!

LÄUFFER: Herr Wenzeslaus!

WENZESLAUS: No more! Not another word! You have shown yourself in your true colors. Out of my house, seducer!

LISE (*kneels down in front of Wenzeslaus*): Dear schoolmaster, he has done me no harm.

WENZESLAUS: He has done you more harm than your worst enemy could do. He has seduced your innocent heart.

LÄUFFER: I confess my guilt . . . but can anyone resist such charms? If you were to tear this heart from my body and mutilate me limb by limb and leave but one artery full of blood, then that one remaining telltale artery would be throbbing still for Lise.

LISE: He has done me no harm.

WENZESLAUS: Done you no harm—Heavenly Father!

LÄUFFER: I have told her she's the most amiable creature ever to rejoice this world of ours. I have impressed that upon her lips. I have sealed with kisses this innocent mouth which otherwise would have seduced me by the magic of its speech into even graver crimes.

WENZESLAUS: Is that not a crime? What do you young gentlemen call crimes these days? *O tempora, O mores!* Have you read your Valerius Maximus? Have you read the article *de pudicitia*? He refers there to a certain Maenius that killed a freed man who once kissed his daughter: and the reason? *Ut etiam oscula ad maritum sincera perferret.* Can you smell that? Can you savor it? *Etiam oscula, non solum virginitatem, etiam oscula.* And Maenius was only a heathen after all: how should a Christian act, who knows that matrimony is instituted by God, and that to poison the bliss of such an institution at the root, to ruin the joy and comfort of a future husband in his spouse, to defile his

heaven . . . Begone, out of my sight! Go to a sultan and
hire yourself to him as foreman in his harem, not a shepherd to my flock. You hireling! You ravening wolf in
sheep's clothing!

LÄUFFER: I wish to marry Lise.

WENZESLAUS: Marry! . . . Oh, to be sure! As if she'd be
satisfied with a eunuch!

LISE: Oh, yes, I'd be perfectly well satisfied, schoolmaster.

LÄUFFER: Unhappy man that I am!

LISE: Believe me, dear schoolmaster, I won't give him up.
I'm fond of him and my heart tells me I cannot be as fond
of anyone else in the whole world as of him.

WENZESLAUS: So . . . but . . . Lise . . . there's something you
don't understand . . . Lise, I can't rightly tell you, but you
can't marry him; it's impossible.

LISE: Why should it be impossible, schoolmaster? How can it
be impossible when I want to, and he wants to, and my
father wants it as well? For my father always used to say
to me, if only I could get a clerical gentleman . . .

WENZESLAUS: But . . . to the dickens with you . . . he can't
do it! May God forgive me my sin, won't you be *told!*

LÄUFFER: Perhaps that isn't what she wants. Lise, I cannot
sleep with you.

LISE: Then you can lie awake with me, if only we're together
during the day and smile at each other and kiss each other's
hands once in a while, for heaven knows I'm fond of him,
I'm fond of you.

LÄUFFER: You see, Herr Wenzeslaus! It's only love she wants
of me. And is it essential for the happiness of a marriage
that animal instincts should be satisfied?

WENZESLAUS: What the . . . ! *Connubium sine prole, est quasi
dies sine sole* . . . Be fruitful and multiply, it says in God's
holy word. Where there is wedlock there must also be
children.

LISE: No, schoolmaster, I swear to you, I would never wish
for children. Children! The things you think of! A fine
thing it would be if I got children into the bargain. My
father has ducks and chickens enough that I have to feed
every day: what if I had to feed children over and above!

LÄUFFER (*kisses her*): Divine Lise!

WENZESLAUS (*drags them apart*): What's this, then. What's this? Before my very eyes? Well, all right, cuddle if you like, for all I care: after all, it is better to marry than to burn. But it's all over between us,. Herr Mandel, all the high hopes I placed in you, all the great expectations your heroism inspired in me . . . Good heavens, how vast after all is the gulf that is fixed between a Father of the Church and a mere capon. I thought he'd be a second Origen—Oh, *homuncio, homuncio*! It would take a very different breed of man to choose on purpose and on principle the path by which he might become a pillar of our foundering Church. A very different breed! Who knows what yet may happen! (*Exit.*)

LÄUFFER: Come with me to your father, Lise! His consent as well, and I shall be the happiest man on earth!

SCENE ELEVEN

Insterburg. PRIVY COUNCILLOR, FRITZ VON BERG, PÄTUS, GUSTCHEN, FRÄULEIN REHAAR. GUSTCHEN *and* FRÄULEIN REHAAR *hide in a closet when the others enter. The* COUNCILLOR *and* FRITZ *hasten toward each other.*

FRITZ (*falls on his knees*): Father!

COUNCILLOR (*raises him to his feet and embraces him*): My son!

FRITZ: Have you forgiven me?

COUNCILLOR: My son!

FRITZ: I am not worthy to be called your son.

COUNCILLOR: Sit down; think no more of it, I pray. But how did you keep yourself in Leipzig? Have you been running up debts again at my expense? No? And how could you afford to leave?

FRITZ: This generous youth paid everything for me.

COUNCILLOR: How was that, then?

PÄTUS: This even more generous . . . Oh, I cannot bring myself to speak . . .

COUNCILLOR: Be seated, children. Speak more clearly. Has your father made it up with you, Herr Pätus?

PÄTUS: I haven't had a line from him.

COUNCILLOR: How did the two of you manage, then?

PÄTUS: A win in the lottery—a trifle—but it came in most useful when we decided to come here.

COUNCILLOR: I see you wild fellows are better natured than your fathers. What can you have thought of me, Fritz? But I was given scandalous accounts of you.

PÄTUS: Seiffenblase, I bet?

COUNCILLOR: I do not care to mention names: that would only give rise to unseemly squabbling that would be out of place here.

PÄTUS: Seiffenblase, or I'll be hanged!

COUNCILLOR: But what brings you back home, Fritz, just at this very moment, when . . .

FRITZ: Continue . . . Oh, that "just this moment," father! The "just this moment" is what I wanted to know.

COUNCILLOR: What then? What then?

FRITZ: Is Gustchen dead?

COUNCILLOR: How now, young lover! What makes you ask?

FRITZ: A letter from Seiffenblase.

COUNCILLOR: He wrote and said that she was dead?

FRITZ: And dishonored, too.

PÄTUS: He's a slanderous rogue!

COUNCILLOR: Do you know a Fräulein Rehaar in Leipzig?

FRITZ: Oh, yes. Her father was my lute teacher.

COUNCILLOR: He meant to dishonor *her*. I saved her from his machinations: that's what's turned him against us.

PÄTUS (*stands up*): Fräulein Rehaar—Devil take him!

COUNCILLOR: Where are you off to?

PÄTUS: Is he in Insterburg?

COUNCILLOR: No, he's not. Don't be too eager to take the part of the princesses, Sir Knight of the Round Table. Or did you know Fräulein Rehaar as well?

PÄTUS: Me? No, I didn't know her . . . yes, I did.

COUNCILLOR: I see. Won't you step into the closet for a moment? (*Leads him to the door.*)

PÄTUS (*opens the door and recoils, clasping his head with both hands*): Fräulein Rehaar! At your feet . . . (*Offstage.*) Can I be so happy? Or is it only a dream? Or delirium? . . . Some enchantment?

COUNCILLOR: Let us leave him. (*Turns to* FRITZ.) Are you still thinking of Gustchen?

FRITZ: You have yet to resolve this dreadful riddle. Was Seiffenblase lying?

COUNCILLOR: I think we can speak of that later; let us not mar our present rapture.

FRITZ (*kneeling*): Oh, father, if you still retain some affection for me, do not leave me hanging thus between heaven and earth, between hope and despair. That is why I came here; I could no longer bear the tormenting uncertainty. Is Gustchen alive? Is it true that she's dishonored?

COUNCILLOR: I fear that's the sad truth.

FRITZ: And she threw herself into a pond?

COUNCILLOR: And her father jumped in after her.

FRITZ: Then let the headsman's ax fall! I am the unhappiest of men.

COUNCILLOR: Stand up! You are innocent of blame.

FRITZ: I shall never stand up again. (*Strikes his chest.*) I was to blame—I alone and no one else. Gustchen, blessed spirit, pardon me!

COUNCILLOR: What have you to reproach yourself with?

FRITZ: I swore an oath, a false oath . . . Gustchen! If only I might follow you! (*Stands up.*) Where's that pond?

COUNCILLOR: Here! (*Leads him to the closet.*)

FRITZ (*offstage, calling out*): Gustchen! Is this a phantom that I see? Heavens, heavens, what rapture! Let me die! Let me expire at your breast!

COUNCILLOR (*wipes his eyes*): A moving spectacle! If only the Major were here! (*Exit.*)

SCENE TWELVE

MAJOR, *a child in his arms;* PÄTUS SENIOR.

MAJOR: Come along, Herr Pätus. You've restored my very

life. That was the only worm that still gnawed at my vitals. I must introduce you to my brother, and I'll have that blind old grandmother of yours framed in gold.

PÄTUS SENIOR: Oh, my mother made me much happier than you by her unexpected visit. You have only regained a grandchild to remind you of melancholy happenings; I have found a mother who recalls to me the happiest scenes of my life and whose maternal affection I was fit to requite, alas, with naught but hatred and ingratitude. I thrust her from my house after she had made over to me the entire estate of my father along with her own fortune. I behaved more savagely toward her than any tiger. What a mercy of God it is that she's still alive, that she can still forgive me, noble saint that she is! That it is within my power to make good my crimes.

MAJOR: Brother Berg! Where are you? Hey! (COUNCILLOR *enters.*) Here is my child, my grandson. Where is Gustchen? My very dearest grandson! (*Caresses the child.*) My very dearest foolish little doll!

COUNCILLOR: Excellent! And you, Herr Pätus?

MAJOR: Herr Pätus recovered the child for me. His mother was the blind old woman, the beggar that Gustchen told us about.

PÄTUS SENIOR: And a beggar because of me. Oh, shame binds my tongue! But I shall tell the whole world what a monster I have been . . .

COUNCILLOR: Have you heard the news, Major? Some suitors for your daughter have turned up—but do not press me for names.

MAJOR: Suitors for my daughter? (*Throws the child on to the sofa.*) Where is she?

COUNCILLOR: Not so fast! Her suitor is with her. Will you give your consent?

MAJOR: Is he of a good house? Is he noble?

COUNCILLOR: I doubt it.

MAJOR: But not too far below her station? Oh, she was to have had the best match in the kingdom. A cursed thought! If I could only be rid of it: it will drive me into bedlam yet.

(COUNCILLOR *opens the closet door; at a sign from him,* FRITZ *emerges with* GUSTCHEN.)

MAJOR (*falls on* FRITZ'*s neck*): Fritz! (*To the* COUNCILLOR.) Is this your Fritz? Do you wish to marry my daughter? God bless you. Have you heard nothing, or have you heard everything? See how my hair has turned grey before its time! (*Leads him to the sofa.*) Look, there is the child. Are you a philosopher? Can you forget everything? Is Gustchen still comely enough for you? Oh, she has repented. Lad, I swear to you, she has repented as no nun or saint ever did. But what's to do? The very angels fell from heaven . . . but Gustchen has risen again.

FRITZ: Allow me to speak.

MAJOR (*still pressing Fritz to his breast*): No, lad, I'd like to squeeze you to death . . . you are so greathearted . . . such noble thoughts . . . that you . . . that you are my very own lad . . .

FRITZ: In Gustchen's arms I envy no king.

MAJOR: Quite right! That's right! She will have confessed to you, she will have told you everything.

FRITZ: This transgression can only make her dearer still to me . . . can only make her heart more angelic . . . she need but look in the mirror to be convinced that she will constitute my entire joy, and yet she trembles at the thought, unbearable to her, so she says, that she might make me unhappy. Oh, what shall I expect from such a woman but a veritable heaven?

MAJOR: A heaven, indeed—if it's true that not only the righteous enter into heaven but also those sinners who repent. My daughter has done penance, and I, too, have repented of my follies and atoned for my failure to listen to a brother who knew better than I did. I have kept her company in that respect; and hence God has made me happy as she is happy.

COUNCILLOR (*calls into the closet*): Herr Pätus, come out. Your father is here.

PÄTUS SENIOR: What do I hear? My son?

PÄTUS (*falls on his father's neck*): Your unhappy son that you disowned. But God looked after me like a poor orphan. Here, papa, is the money that you spent for my education abroad. Here you have it back, and my thanks as well. It has borne double interest: the capital has increased and your son has turned out an honest fellow.

PÄTUS SENIOR: Must you all vie with each other today in putting me to shame by your noble deeds? My son, know once again your father, who for a time cast off his human nature and sank to the level of a savage beast. Your grandmother has fared as you have: she, too, has returned and forgiven me and has made me her son once more, just as you have made me your father again. Take my entire fortune, Gustav! Apply it as you will, but do not make me suffer for the ingratitude I displayed to your grandmother when she made me a similar bequest.

PÄTUS: Permit me to render happy with this fortune the sweetest and most virtuous of maidens.

PÄTUS SENIOR: What then? You two in love? I am only too glad to grant you whatever you please. I am old and would like before I die to see grandchildren to whom I might show the fidelity your grandmother has shown toward me.

FRITZ (*embraces the child on the sofa, kisses it and carries it over to* GUSTCHEN): This child is now mine as well—a melancholy pledge of the frailties of your sex and the folly of ours—most of all, however, of the advantages of the education of young ladies by private tutors.

MAJOR: Yes, my dear son, but how shall they be educated, then?

COUNCILLOR: Are there no institutions, no sewing schools, no convents, no educational establishments? But we'll talk of that another time.

FRITZ (*kisses the child again*): And yet infinitely dear to me because it bears the likeness of its mother. At least, sweet boy, I'll never have you educated by private tutors!

(*Curtain.*)

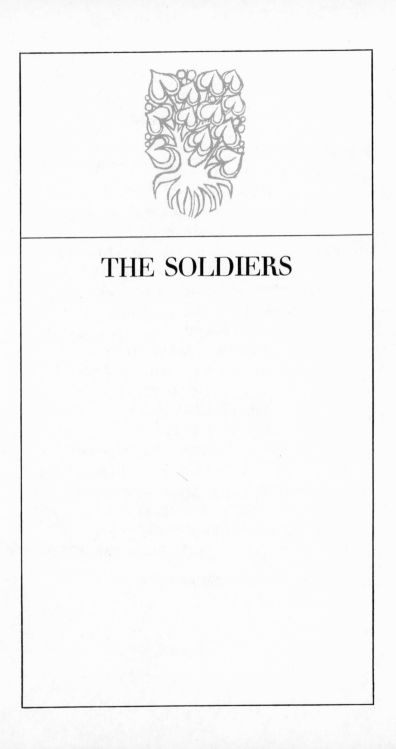

THE SOLDIERS

CAST
(in order of appearance)

MARIE WESENER ⎫
CHARLOTTE WESENER ⎬ daughters of Monsieur Wesener

SERVANT

STOLZIUS, cloth merchant in Armentières

HIS MOTHER

DESPORTES, a nobleman from Hainaut in French service

WESENER, fancy-goods dealer in Lille

COUNT VON SPANNHEIM, Desportes' colonel

EISENHARDT, regimental chaplain

COUNT DE LA ROCHE, cousin of Spannheim

HIS TUTOR · MAJOR HAUDY

LIEUTENANT MURRAY · MADAME WESENER

MAID · CAPTAIN PIRZEL

LIEUTENANT RAMMLER

MADEMOISELLE ZIPFERSAAT

WESENER'S MOTHER · AARON, a Jew

COUNTESS DE LA ROCHE, mother of the young Count

FOOTMAN · DESPORTES' GAMEKEEPER

GILBERT · MADAME BISCHOF

MADEMOISELLE BISCHOF, her cousin

LADIES, GENTLEMEN, OFFICERS, BYSTANDERS etc.

The play takes place in Flanders.

ACT ONE

SCENE ONE

Lille. MARIE, CHARLOTTE.

MARIE (*with her chin in her hand, writing a letter*): Sister, do you know how to spell "Madame"? *M—a—d: Mad; d—a—m: dam; m—e: me.*

CHARLOTTE (*sitting and spinning*): That's right.

MARIE: Listen, I'll read it to you, and you say if it's all right: "Dear madame. We've arrived safe back in Lille, thank goodness." Is that right, "arrived": *a—r: ar; e—i—v—d: rived:* arrived?

CHARLOTTE: That's right.

MARIE: "We cannot think how we have merited the kindness with which you overwhelmed us, wish, however, we were so situated . . ." Is that correct?

CHARLOTTE: Read on to the end of the sentence, can't you?

MARIE: "As to repay your esteemed courtesy and favors, but seeing as it isn't in our power, can only crave continuation of same."

CHARLOTTE: *We* can only crave.

MARIE: Oh, leave me alone, do! Why must you keep interrupting?

CHARLOTTE: *We* can only crave continuation of same.

MARIE: Oh, why do you go on so? Papa writes like that too, you know. (*Folds the letter and prepares to seal it.*)

CHARLOTTE: Well, finish reading, then.

MARIE: The rest is none of your business. You always want to make out you're smarter than papa: only the other day papa said it wasn't polite to keep writing "we" and "I" and all that. (*Seals the letter.*) Here, Steffen, (*gives the servant money*) take this letter to the post.

CHARLOTTE: It's just that you didn't want to read me the last bit; I expect you've put something nice in it for Monsieur Stolzius.

MARIE: That's none of your business.

CHARLOTTE: Well, I never! Do you think I'm jealous, then? I could have written just as well as you, but I didn't want to take away from you the pleasure of showing off your fine hand.

MARIE: Listen, Lottie, stop teasing me about Stolzius, or else I'll go straight down and complain to papa.

CHARLOTTE: Well, just think of that! What do I care: he knows anyway that you're in love with him, and you can't bear anyone else even to mention his name.

MARIE: Lottie! (*Bursts into tears and runs downstairs.*)

SCENE TWO

Armentières. STOLZIUS *and his* MOTHER.

STOLZIUS (*with a bandage round his head*): I'm not well, mother.

MOTHER (*stands for a moment looking at him*): Well, I do believe you've got that wretched girl stuck in your head, that's why it hurts so much. You haven't had a cheerful moment since she went away.

STOLZIUS: Seriously, mother, there's something not right with me.

MOTHER: Well, if you speak nicely to me, perhaps I can cheer you up a little. (*Takes a letter from her pocket.*)

STOLZIUS (*jumps to his feet.*) She's written to you . . . !

MOTHER: Here, you can read it. (STOLZIUS *snatches the letter from her hand and pores over it.*) But listen, the Colonel wants that cloth measured out for the regiments.

STOLZIUS: Let me answer the letter, mother.

MOTHER: I'm talking about the cloth, Tom Noddy, that the Colonel ordered for the regiments. Come along . . .

SCENE THREE

Lille. MARIE, DESPORTES.

DESPORTES: What are you doing there, divine mademoiselle?

MARIE (*has a pile of blank paper in front of her on which she is scribbling, quickly puts her pen behind her ear*): Oh, nothing, nothing, sir. (*Smiling.*) I'm far too fond of writing.

DESPORTES: If only I were so happy as to see one of your letters, even a single line from your fair hand.

MARIE: Oh, I beg your pardon. I don't have a fair hand, I'm quite ashamed to show you anything I've written.

DESPORTES: Anything that comes from such a hand is bound to be fair.

MARIE: Oh, Baron, pray stop. I know that these are simply empty compliments.

DESPORTES (*kneeling down*): I swear to you, never in all my life have I beheld a being more perfect than you, mademoiselle.

MARIE (*knitting, with her eyes fixed on her work*): My mother told me, you know . . . Look how two-faced you are.

DESPORTES: Two-faced! Me? Can you believe that of me, divine mademoiselle? Is it two-faced to sneak away from my regiment, having sold my tour of duty, and risk being thrown into jail when I return, if they find out I'm not with my parents, as I said I was? Is that two-faced? Just to have the bliss of seeing you, my paragon!

MARIE (*looking down at her work again*): But mother has often told me I'm not properly grown up yet, I'm at an age when girls are neither pretty nor homely.

WESENER (*enters*): Well, well, look who's here! Your humble servant, Baron. How come we have the honor of your presence once again? (*Embraces him.*)

DESPORTES: I'm only here for a week or two to visit a relative of mine who has come up from Brussels.

WESENER: I'm sorry I wasn't at home. My little Marie will have bored you, I fear. How are your esteemed parents; I hope they received the snuffboxes?

DESPORTES: No doubt. I haven't been home. I expect we have another account to settle, Wesener?

WESENER: Oh, time enough for that; it isn't the first time, after all. Your lady mother didn't come down for our carnival last winter.

DESPORTES: She is not too well. Were there many dances?

WESENER: So, so, a fair number. You know I never go to any, and my daughters neither.

DESPORTES: But is it fair, Wesener, to deny your daughters all such pleasures? Is it healthy to do that?

WESENER: Oh, if they work hard they'll be healthy enough. There's nothing the matter with my little Marie, thank heaven, and she always has fine pink cheeks.

MARIE: Yes, papa won't hear different, and sometimes I get such a tight feeling sitting indoors that I don't know what to do with myself. I feel so on edge.

DESPORTES: You see, you allow your daughter no entertainments, and that will turn her melancholic one of these days.

WESENER: Nonsense, she has entertainment enough with her friends; when the lot of them get together you can't hear yourself speak.

DESPORTES: Allow me the honor of escorting your daughter to the theater some time. They're giving a new piece today.

MARIE: Oh, papa!

WESENER: No! No, definitely not, Baron! I trust you will not take it amiss, but my daughter is not in the habit of going to the play: it would only cause talk among the neighbors— and with a young gentleman from the military, at that!

DESPORTES: You can see I'm in civilian dress. Who will recognize me?

WESENER: So much the worse! Once for all, it's not a proper thing with any young gentleman, whoever he may be. She's not even been confirmed yet, and she should go to the theater and act the grand lady! In short, Baron, I'll not allow it.

MARIE: But, papa, if nobody knows the Baron by sight.

WESENER (*sotto voce*): Hold your tongue, can't you? Nobody knows him? So much the worse if nobody knows him. Your pardon, Baron, gladly as I'd do you the favor . . . in all other matters I am at your service.

DESPORTES: By the way, my dear Wesener, won't you show me some of your brooches, please?

WESENER: At once! (*Exit.*)

DESPORTES: Shall I tell you something, my angel, my divine Marie? We'll play a trick on your father. We can't do it today, but the day after tomorrow they're putting on a splendid piece, *La chercheuse d'esprit,* and the curtain raiser is *Le déserteur.* Haven't you a good friend somewhere here?

MARIE: Frau Weyher.

DESPORTES: Where does she live?

MARIE: Right on the corner by the fountain.

DESPORTES: I'll go there, and you come too, and then we'll go off to the play together. (*Wesener returns with a large cardboard box full of brooches.* MARIE *smiles and makes a sign to* DESPORTES.)

WESENER: Here you are: all different prices. This one's 100 livres, this one's 50, and this one's 150.

DESPORTES (*inspects one after the other and shows the box to* MARIE): Which would you recommend? (MARIE *smiles, and as soon as her father is engrossed in unpacking the brooches, she makes signs to* DESPORTES.)

WESENER: Look, this one sparkles splendidly, 'pon my word.

DESPORTES: You're right. (*Holds it up beside* MARIE's *head.*) Look at that against such lovely brown hair, what a splendid effect! Listen, Monsieur Wesener, it suits your daughter so well, won't you be so kind as to let her keep it?

WESENER (*hands back the brooch with a smile*): Pardon me, Baron, but that would never do . . . my daughter has never in her life accepted presents from gentlemen.

MARIE (*her eyes fixed on her knitting*): I couldn't have worn it anyway; it's much too big for my hairstyle.

DESPORTES: Then I'll send it to my mother. (*Wraps up the brooch carefully.*)

WESENER (*wrapping up the remaining brooches, mutters something to* MARIE): You're just a trinket yourself! You'll never wear a thing like that on your head, that's no fashion for the likes of you. (*She says nothing and goes on with her knitting.*)

DESPORTES: I'll take my leave then, Monsieur Wesener!
We'll settle up before I go.

WESENER: Time enough for that, Baron, time enough for that.
Be so kind as to honor us with another visit some time.

DESPORTES: By your leave. Farewell, Mademoiselle Marie!
(*Exit.*)

MARIE: Well I never, papa, how you do go on!

WESENER: I've gone and done something not to your liking
again, eh? What do you know of the world, you silly chick.

MARIE: He's a real good-hearted gentleman, the Baron.

WESENER: Because he pays you a few compliments and all that
sort of thing. One's as bad as the next, and don't you try to
tell me anything about the young gentry of the military.
They're in and out of all the inns and coffeehouses telling
each other tales, and before you know where you are, a poor
girl is the talk of the town. Yes, and Mademoiselle this or
Mademoiselle that is no better than she ought to be, and I
know of this one and that one, and she'd like to have him
where she wants him . . .

MARIE: Papa! (*Begins to weep.*) You're always so coarse!

WESENER (*pats* MARIE's *cheek*): You mustn't mind me. You're
my only joy, you little fool, that's why I worry about you.

MARIE: If only you'd let me worry about myself. After all, I'm
not a child any more.

SCENE FOUR

Armentières. COUNT VON SPANNHEIM (the COLONEL)
at table with his chaplain, EISENHARDT; *the* COLONEL's
cousin, a YOUNG COUNT; *the* YOUNG COUNT's TUTOR;
MAJOR HAUDY; MURRAY *and other officers.*

YOUNG COUNT: Do you think we shall have a good troupe of
actors here again soon?

HAUDY: It would be highly desirable, especially for our
younger gentlemen. They say Godeau meant to come to
Armentières.

TUTOR: In truth, it can't be denied, the stage is a well-nigh indispensable amenity for a garrison, *c'est-à-dire* a stage on which good taste prevails, as for example the French stage.

EISENHARDT: I cannot see the benefit of it.

COLONEL: You're saying that, chaplain, simply because you have those two white tabs there under your chin. I know you really think otherwise in your heart of hearts.

EISENHARDT: I beg your pardon, Colonel. I've never been a hypocrite, and if that were a necessary vice for our calling, then I imagine army chaplains at least would be exempt from it, since they have to do with the more sensible sort of men. I am fond of the theater myself and I like to go and watch a good play, but I do not for that reason believe it is such a beneficial institution for the officer corps.

HAUDY: For God's sake, parson or preacher or whatever you call yourself, just you tell me what excesses are not forestalled or prevented by the theater. After all, officers must have some pastime or other.

EISENHARDT: No need to be so heated, Major! Say, rather, what excesses have not been instigated among officers by the theater.

HAUDY: Nothing but talk and, what's more, beside the point. In short, sir, (*plants both elbows on the table and leans forward*) I tell you here and now, a single play—even supposing it were the worst sort of farce—promotes more benefit, not only among officers but in the nation as a whole, than all the sermons that you and your like have ever preached or are ever likely to preach.

COLONEL (*angrily*): Major!

EISENHARDT: If I labored under some prejudice in favor of my office, Major, I would lose my temper. But as it is, let us leave all that aside, for I do not reckon you or many of these gentlemen capable of judging aright the proper function of our office as long as you live. Let us confine ourselves to the theater and the amazing benefits it is alleged to have for the gentlemen of the corps. Pray, answer me one question: what do these gentlemen learn from the theater?

MURRAY: Oh, Lord, do we always have to be learning something? We enjoy ourselves, isn't that enough?

EISENHARDT: Would to God that you *did* only enjoy yourselves, that you *didn't* learn anything! But in fact you emulate what is represented on the stage and inflict calamity and blight upon our families.

COLONEL: My dear chaplain, your zeal is praiseworthy, but it smacks of the cassock, if you don't mind my saying so. What family has ever been ruined by an officer? No doubt a wench or two that deserves no better is put in the family way.

HAUDY: A whore will always turn out a whore, no matter whose hands she falls into; if not a soldier's whore, then a preacher's whore.

EISENHARDT: It vexes me, Major, that you keep on dragging preachers into the argument because it prevents me from answering you in a really forthright way. You might imagine something of personal rancor in what I say, and if I grow heated it's due to the subject of our discourse, not to your sneers and insults concerning my office. That can neither gain nor lose by all your witty conceits.

HAUDY: Talk, talk, talk; blather away! That's what we're here for, who's stopping you?

EISENHARDT: What you were saying a moment ago is an idea worthy of the soul of a Nero or an Oglei-Oglu—which even in such a context might have aroused horror when it was first stated. A whore will always turn out a whore! Are you so intimately acquainted with the opposite sex?

HAUDY: You're not the man to instruct me, sir.

EISENHARDT: You owe your acquaintance with them to the masterpieces of your art, perhaps, but permit me to inform you, a whore will never turn out a whore unless someone makes her a whore. The urge is in all human creatures, but every female knows that she owes her entire future happiness to this urge, and will she sacrifice that if she is not tricked into it?

HAUDY: Am I talking about respectable girls?

EISENHARDT: It is precisely the respectable girls who are bound to tremble at your plays. That's where you acquire the art of destroying their respectability.

MURRAY: Who would harbor such evil thoughts!

HAUDY: You've a damned uncivil tongue when you speak of officers, sir. God damn it, if anyone else were to talk to me like that . . .! Do you think, sir, we cease to be gentlemen the moment we enter the service?

EISENHARDT: I wish you much joy of your convictions. But as long as I observe kept mistresses and the ruined daughters of respectable families, then I cannot retract my opinion.

HAUDY: That deserves a punch on the nose!

EISENHARDT (*stands up*): Sir, I, too, bear a sword!

COLONEL: Major, please! Pastor Eisenhardt is not at fault, what do you expect of him? And the first man who offends him . . . be seated, chaplain, he shall give you satisfaction. (*Exit* HAUDY.) But you go too far, Pastor Eisenhardt, all the same. There's not an officer who doesn't know full well what honor requires of him.

EISENHARDT: If he has time enough to think of it. But in our latest plays isn't it the case that the most dastardly crimes against the hallowed rights of fathers and families are represented in such glowing colors, the most venomous deeds rendered so innocuous that a villain stands before us as if he'd come straight down from heaven? Is that not calculated to encourage, is it not calculated to stifle every scruple conscience may have assimilated from the parental home? Deceiving a watchful father, instructing an innocent maiden in the practice of the vices—these are the tasks accomplished and rewarded on the stage.

HAUDY (*in the entrance hall with other officers, as the door opens momentarily*): That confounded preacher . . .

COLONEL: Let's be off to the coffeehouse, chaplain, you still owe me my revenge at chess . . . And, adjutant, would you request Major Haudy not to leave his quarters today. Tell him, I shall return his sword to him personally tomorrow.

SCENE FIVE

Lille. WESENER *sitting at supper with* MADAME WESENER *and* CHARLOTTE, *their elder daughter.* MARIE *enters, dressed in all her finery.*

MARIE (*throws her arms round her father's neck*): Oh, papa, papa!

WESENER (*with his mouth full*): What is it, what's the matter with you?

MARIE: I cannot keep it secret from you: I've been to the play. What a thing it is, to be sure!

(WESENER *pushes his chair back from the table and turns away his face.*)

MARIE: If only you'd seen what I've seen, you wouldn't be angry, papa. (*Sits on his lap.*) Dear papa, such goings-on, it was, I shan't be able to sleep all night, it was such fun! The Baron *is* kind!

WESENER: What? It was the Baron that took you to the play?

MARIE (*somewhat timidly*): Yes, papa, dear papa!

WESENER (*shoves her off his lap*): Away with you, you hussy! Do you mean to become the Baron's mistress?

MARIE (*with her face half turned away, half weeping*): I was at Madame Weyher's . . . and we were standing at the door . . . (*stammering*) and then he spoke to us.

WESENER: Yes, go on, lie! Lie the Devil's ear off! Out of my sight, you godless creature!

CHARLOTTE: I could have told papa it would come to this. They've been carrying on together on the quiet all the time, the Baron and her.

MARIE (*weeping*): Hold your tongue, can't you!

CHARLOTTE: Well, I never! Not for you, I won't! Tries to order people about and carries on the way she does . . .

MARIE: You just watch yourself, you and that young Monsieur Heidevogel of yours. If I behaved half as bad as you . . .

WESENER: Will you be quiet, both of you! Go to your room this instant, you shan't have any supper, you wicked creature! (*Exit* MARIE.) And you be quiet, too, I don't suppose you're any angel either. Do you think no one sees why Monsieur Heidevogel comes here so often?

CHARLOTTE: It's all Marie's fault. (*Weeps.*) The God-forsaken strumpet, she just wants to get decent girls into trouble because that's the way her own mind works.

WESENER (*very loudly*): Hold your tongue! Marie is far too high-minded to talk about you like that, but you're jealous of your own sister. Seeing you haven't her looks you might at least have a more respectable way of thinking. Shame on you! (*To the maid*). Take it away, I can't eat any more. (*Pushes away his plate and napkin, throws himself into an armchair, and sits plunged in thought.*)

SCENE SIX

MARIE's *bedroom.* MARIE *is sitting on her bed, has the brooch in her hand, and is looking at herself in a mirror, lost in thought. Her father comes in, she gives a start and tries to hide the brooch.*

MARIE: Oh, Lord!

WESENER: Now then, don't be such a child. (*Strides up and down the room a couple of times, then sits down beside* MARIE.) Listen, Marie! You know I'm fond of you, be frank with me; it will not be to your disadvantage. Tell me, has the Baron said anything to you about love?

MARIE (*with an air of mystery*): Papa! He's in love with me, he really is. Just look: he gave me this brooch.

WESENER: What the dickens! Damn it all! (*Takes the brooch from her.*) Didn't I tell you not to . . .

MARIE: But, papa, I can't be so rude and refuse him. I can tell you, he carried on like a madman when I said I wouldn't take it. (*Goes over to the cabinet.*) Here are some verses he wrote about me. (*Gives him a piece of paper.*)

WESENER (*reading aloud*):

> Sublimest object of my chastest passion soaring,
> I cannot cease from loving thee, adoring
> With never-dying faithfulness imbued
> This fairest orb of day with ev'ry morn renewed.

"This fairest orb of day"—ha, ha, ha!

MARIE: Wait, I'll show you something else. He gave me a little heart, too, set with stones in a ring. (*Goes back to the cabinet and takes out the ring. Her father glances at it carelessly.*)

WESENER (*reads again*): "Sublimest object of my chastest passion soaring." His intentions are honorable, I can see that. But listen, Marie, mark what I say. You mustn't accept any more presents from him. I don't like him giving you all these presents.

MARIE: It's his kind heart, papa.

WESENER: And give me that brooch. I'll give it back to him. Leave it to me, I know what's good for you. I've lived longer in this world than you have, my girl, and you can go to the theater with him again, but take Madame Weyher with you and don't let on that I know about it. Tell him he must keep it dark and that I would be very angry if I knew. But for heaven's sake, girl, take no more presents from him.

MARIE: I know my papa wouldn't give me bad advice. (*Kisses his hand.*) You'll see, I'll follow your advice to the letter. And I'll tell you everything, you can depend on it.

WESENER: Well, all right, then. (*Kisses her.*) You might end up a real lady yet, you silly child. You never know your luck.

MARIE (*in a subdued tone*): But papa—what will poor Stolzius say?

WESENER: You mustn't scare off Stolzius right away, d'you hear? Now, I'll tell you how to word your letter to him. In the meantime sleep well, you little monkey.

MARIE (*kisses his hand*): Good night, Pappushka! (*When her father has gone she sighs deeply and goes to the window, unlacing her bodice.*) My heart is so heavy. I do believe we shall have thunder tonight. If the lightning were to strike... (*Casts her eyes up to heaven, places her hands on her breast.*) Dear God, what have I done wrong, then? Stolzius ... I love you still ... but if I can make my fortune ... and papa himself advises me to ... (*Pulls the curtain to.*) If it strikes, then it strikes: I'd not be sorry to die. (*Blows out the lamp.*)

ACT TWO

SCENE ONE

Armentières. HAUDY *and* STOLZIUS *walking by the River Lys.*

HAUDY: You mustn't let yourself be bullied right from the start, my dear friend! I know Desportes; he's a scoundrel who's only out to enjoy himself. But that doesn't necessarily mean he's out to lure away your fiancée.

STOLZIUS: But the gossip, Major! The town is full of it and all the countryside as well for miles around. I could jump into the river this minute just to think of it!

HAUDY (*takes his arm*): You mustn't take it so much to heart. The Devil knows, everybody has to put up with gossip! I'm your best friend, you can be sure of that, and I'd certainly tell you if there was any danger. But there is none, you're just imagining it. Make sure, though, that the wedding can take place this winter, while we're still in garrison here, and if Desportes causes you the slightest trouble, I'll have his blood, I promise you. Meanwhile, take no notice of the gossip; you must know that the most respectable girls are most talked about; it's natural that the young idiots who haven't had their way with them should try to get their own back.

SCENE TWO

Coffeehouse. EISENHARDT *and* PIRZEL *on a sofa in the foreground, drinking coffee. In the background a group of officers chatting and laughing.*

EISENHARDT (*to* PIRZEL): It's laughable the way people swarm round that poor Stolzius like flies round a honeypot. One plucks at him here, another nudges him there, this one goes walking with him, that one takes him into his cabriolet, another plays billiards with him: like bloodhounds on the scent! And how remarkably his cloth trade has prospered since it became known that he's to marry the good-looking young lady who passed through here not long ago.

PIRZEL (*seizes* EISENHARDT's *hand, vehemently*): Why is that, pastor? Because people don't think! (*Strikes a highly picturesque pose, half turned toward the group in the background.*) A perfect Being exists. Either I can insult this perfect Being—or else I cannot insult Him.

ONE OF THE GROUP (*turning round*): Off again, is he?

PIRZEL (*eagerly*): If I can insult Him, (*turns to the group*) then He would cease to be the most perfect Being.

ANOTHER OF THE GROUP: Yes, indeed, Pirzel, you're absolutely right, absolutely right.

PIRZEL (*turns quickly to* EISENHARDT): If I cannot insult Him ... (*Seizes his hand and stands quite motionless in deep thought.*)

TWO OR THREE OF THE GROUP: Hang it all, Pirzel, are you speaking to us?

PIRZEL (*turns solemnly toward them*): My dear comrades, you are venerable creations of God, hence I cannot but respect you and venerate you; I, too, am God's creation, so you must hold me equally in respect.

ONE OF THE GROUP: If you take our advice, you'll do just that!

PIRZEL (*turns again to the chaplain*): Now ...

EISENHARDT: Captain, I am entirely of your opinion on every point. Only the question was, how can we get it into people's heads that they should leave poor Stolzius in peace and not cast jealousy and suspicion into two hearts that otherwise might have rendered each other eternally happy.

PIRZEL (*who has meanwhile sat down, jumps up again hastily*): As I had the honor and pleasure of telling you, chaplain, that's because people simply don't think. Think, think what man is—that's what I say. (*Seizes his hand.*) Look, that's your hand, but what is it, in fact? Skin, bones, clay! (*Taps *his pulse.*) There, there, that's where it is—this is just the sheath, the blade's in there, in the blood, in the blood . . . (*Looks round suddenly because of the commotion caused by* HAUDY, *who enters shouting at the top of his voice.*)

HAUDY: I've got him, boys! He's as mild as mother's milk! (*Roars at the top of his voice.*) Madame Roux! Get some glasses rinsed and brew us a good punch! He'll be here any moment. Do me a favor and treat the fellow courteously.

EISENHARDT (*leans forward*): Who, Major, if I may ask?

HAUDY (*without looking at him*): Nothing: a good friend of mine.

(*The whole company throngs around* HAUDY.)

AN OFFICER: Have you quizzed him? Will the wedding be soon?

HAUDY: You must let me handle this, fellows, otherwise you'll queer my pitch. He trusts me, I tell you, like the prophet Daniel, and if any of you puts his oar in, then the whole thing's screwed up. He's jealous enough as it is, poor soul; Desportes has given him a cruel lot to think about, and it took me all my time to stop him jumping into the river. My dodge is to make him trust the woman; he must know her and realize she's not one of the impregnable kind. That's just to let you know, so you don't put the man off.

RAMMLER: What are you talking about! I know him better than you do, he's got a pretty sharp nose, believe you me!

HAUDY: And you've got an even sharper one, I can see.

RAMMLER: You think the way to get into his good books is to say flattering things about his fiancée. You're wrong: I know him better, it's just the opposite. He pretends to believe you, takes note of everything you say, and never lets on. But if we can make him suspicious of the woman, he'll think we're being open and above board with him . . .

HAUDY: You and your airy-fairy schemes! D'you want to send the fellow crazy? Don't you think he's got enough maggots in his head as it is? And if he leaves her in the lurch, or strings himself up—where are you then? A man's life is no bagatelle, is it, chaplain?

EISENHARDT: I want no part in your council of war.

HAUDY: But you must admit I'm right.

PIRZEL: My worthy brothers and comrades, do no man wrong. A man's life is a legacy with which he is endowed. But no one has the right to dispose of a legacy bestowed on him by someone else. Our life is such a legacy . . .

HAUDY (*seizes* PIRZEL *by the hand*): Yes, Pirzel, you're the finest fellow I know! (*Sits down between* PIRZEL *and* EISENHARDT.) But the Jesuit here, (*embraces* EISENHARDT) he's itching to be cock of the walk himself . . .

RAMMLER (*sits down on* EISENHARDT'*s other side and whispers in his ear*): Chaplain, you'll see what a trick I'll play on Haudy. (STOLZIUS *enters.* HAUDY *jumps up.*)

HAUDY: Ah, my dear fellow, come along! I've ordered a good glass of punch for the two of us. That wind went through us like a knife. (*Leads him to a table.*)

STOLZIUS (*taking off his hat, to the others*): Gentlemen, you'll pardon my being so bold as to come to your coffeehouse; it was on the Major's insistence.

(*They all take off their hats politely and bow. Rammler gets up and comes over to join* HAUDY *and* STOLZIUS.)

RAMMLER: Your humble servant: we're signally honored!

STOLZIUS (*raises his hat once more, rather distantly, and sits down beside* HAUDY): There's such a bitter wind out there, I do believe we shall have snow.

HAUDY: I believe so, too. (*Filling a pipe.*) You do smoke, don't you, Monsieur Stolzius?

STOLZIUS: A little.

RAMMLER: I can't think what's happened to our punch, Haudy. (*Stands up.*) What can that confounded Roux woman be doing all this time.

HAUDY: Mind your own business! (*Shouts at the top of his voice.*) Madame Roux! Bring some candles! And our punch—where is it?

STOLZIUS: Oh, Major, I should be heartily sorry to cause you any inconvenience.

HAUDY: Not a bit of it, dear friend. (*Offers him the pipe.*) Truly, that breeze off the Lys does one no good at all!

RAMMLER (*sits down at their table*): Have you had any word from Lille lately? How is your fiancée? (HAUDY *glares at him;* RAMMLER *remains seated with a bland smile on his face.*)

STOLZIUS (*in embarrassment*): I . . . humbly beg your pardon, sir . . . I know nothing of a fiancée, I haven't one.

RAMMLER: Mademoiselle Wesener from Lille, is she not your intended? Desportes wrote and told me you were betrothed.

STOLZIUS: Then Monsieur Desportes must know more of the matter than I do.

HAUDY (*smoking*): Rammler is never done jabbering: he's no idea what he's talking about or what he's after.

ONE OF THE GROUP: I assure you, Monsieur Stolzius, Desportes is a man of honor.

STOLZIUS: I never doubted it in the least.

HAUDY: A fat lot you people know about Desportes, I must say. If anyone knows him, then it's me for sure. His mother put him under my wing when he joined the regiment, and he's never yet done anything without consulting me. But I assure you, Monsieur Stolzius, Desportes is a man of feeling and religion.

RAMMLER: We were schoolmates together. Never seen a man in my life who was so shy with women.

HAUDY: That's true, he's right there. Desportes is incapable of uttering a single word the moment a female gives him an encouraging look.

RAMMLER (*adopting a studied air of guilelessness*): I do believe, in fact—if I'm not mistaken—yes, it's true, he still writes to her . . . on the very day of his departure I read a letter he had written to a young lady in Brussels, a girl he was quite astonishingly infatuated with. He will probably marry her quite soon, I should think.

ONE OF THE GROUP: The only thing I can't make out is what he's doing in Lille all this time.

HAUDY: God damn it! What's happened to our punch? Madame Roux!

RAMMLER: In Lille! Oh, I'm the only one who can explain that, for I'm privy to all his secrets. But it's not something I care to say in public.

HAUDY (*irritably*): Spit it out, you fool! What are you trying to hide it for?

RAMMLER (*laughing*): I can only say so much: he's waiting for a certain person there he means to clear off with on the quiet.

STOLZIUS (*stands up and lays down the pipe*): Gentlemen, I beg to take my leave of you.

HAUDY (*startled*): What's this? Where are you off to, my dear friend? We shall have our punch any minute now.

STOLZIUS: Please do not be offended, but something has just come over me all of a sudden.

HAUDY: But what? The punch will do you good, I assure you.

STOLZIUS: I do not feel well, my dear Major. You will excuse me . . . permit me . . . but I cannot stay here a moment longer, or else I shall faint . . .

HAUDY: It's the Rhine air—or was the tobacco too strong?

STOLZIUS: Good-bye! (*Exit, swaying on his feet.*)

HAUDY: That's done it! You shitheads!

RAMMLER: Ha, ha, ha! (*Thinks for a moment, striding about the room.*) You stupid devils, didn't you see I fixed it all on purpose? What did I tell you, chaplain?

EISENHARDT: Leave me out of this sport, I beg of you!

HAUDY: You scheming cockatoo! I'll wring your neck!

RAMMLER: And I'll smash your arms and legs and chuck them out of the window! (*Struts about in melodramatic fashion.*) You don't know what dodges I've still got up my sleeve.

HAUDY: Yes, you're full of dodges like an old sheepskin's full of lice. You make me sick with your scheming!

RAMMLER: And I'll wager I'm more than a match for the whole bunch of you here when it comes to Stolzius, if I once put my mind to it.

HAUDY: Listen, Rammler! You've got more wit than is good for you; you're too clever by half. You're like a bottle that's filled too full: when you turn it upside down, not a single drop comes out because they're all jammed together. Get away with you: when I have a wife I'll give you leave to bed with her—if you can talk her into it.

RAMMLER (*striding rapidly up and down*): You'll see, the lot of you, what I make of that Stolzius! (*Exit.*)

HAUDY: The fellow gives me the bellyache with his fool ideas. All he can do is wreck other people's plans.

ONE OF THE GROUP: That's true. He has his finger in every pie.

MURRAY: He's always got his head stuffed with plots and crafty schemes; he thinks other people are as incapable of living

without such things as he is. Not long ago I happened to ask
Reitz privately whether he wouldn't lend me his spurs for the
following day. If he didn't chase me around for the rest of the
day, begging me for God's sake to tell him what we meant
to do! I do believe there's a statesman gone to waste in him!

ANOTHER OFFICER: The other day I stopped in front of a house
to read a letter in the shade. He jumped to the conclusion it
was a love letter that had been thrown down to me and kept
on prowling round the house until midnight. I thought I'd
split my sides! There's an old Jew of sixty lives in the house,
and Rammler had posted sentries all over the place to spy
on me and give him a signal if I went in. I bribed one of the
fellows, and he told me the whole thing for three livres. I
thought I'd die laughing!

ALL: Ha, ha, ha! And he thought there was a pretty girl in the
house!

MURRAY: Listen! If you want a good laugh, let's warn the Jew
that there's someone prowling around with an eye on his
ducats.

HAUDY: That's an idea! Come on, let's go right away. It will
be a riot! And you, Murray, put it into his head that the
most beautiful woman in all Armentières lives there and
that Gilbert told you in confidence he was going to pay her a
visit tonight.

SCENE THREE

Lille. MARIE *in an armchair, weeping, a letter in her hand.*
Enter DESPORTES.

DESPORTES: What's wrong, my golden Marie, what's the matter with you?

MARIE (*tries to hide the letter in her pocket*): Oh!

DESPORTES: For heaven's sake, what sort of letter is that to
cause you such tears?

MARIE (*more composed*): Just look at what that fellow Stolzius
has written: as if he had a right to scold me! (*Weeps again.*)

DESPORTES (*reads the letter silently*): The impertinent ass!
But tell me, why do you correspond with such a cur?

MARIE (*dries her eyes*): I can only say, Baron, it's because he's asked for my hand, and I'm half promised to him.

DESPORTES: Asked for your hand? How dare he! Wait, I'll give that ass an answer to his letter.

MARIE: Yes, my dear Baron! And you wouldn't believe what I have to put up with from father; he's never done telling me I oughn't to spurn my good fortune.

DESPORTES: Your good fortune? With a lout like that? What can you be thinking of, my dearest Marie—and what can your father be thinking of? I know the man and his circumstances, as it happens. To put it in a nutshell; you're not cut out to marry a commoner.

MARIE: No, Baron, nothing will come of all this! Those are simply vain hopes you're trying to beguile me with. Your family will never consent to it.

DESPORTES: That is my concern. Do you have pen and ink? I'll reply to the cur's letter, just you wait!

MARIE: No, I'll write myself. (*Sits down at the table and arranges writing materials*; DESPORTES *comes and stands at her shoulder.*)

DESPORTES: Then I'll dictate to you.

MARIE: No, you shan't. (*Writes.*)

DESPORTES (*reading over her shoulder*): "Monsieur . . ." Bumpkin, put there. (*Dips a pen in the inkwell, and makes as if to write.*)

MARIE (*covering the paper with her arms.*) Baron!

(*They begin to tease each other; as soon as she takes her arm away, he makes as if to write. After much laughter she smears his face with the pen. He runs over to the mirror to wipe the ink off, she goes on writing.*)

DESPORTES: I've still got my eye on you.

(*He comes nearer, she threatens him with her pen, finally she puts the paper away in her pocket. He tries to stop her and they wrestle with each other.* MARIE *tickles* DESPORTES, *he begins to yell at the top of his voice and finally falls breathlessly into an armchair.*)

WESENER (*enters*): Now, then, what's all this? We'll have people in from the street any moment, at this rate.

MARIE (*getting her breath back*): Papa, just imagine what kind of letter that ill-bred lout Stolzius has written to me. He calls me an unfaithful girl! Just think, as if we'd herded pigs together. But I'll give him the sort of answer he doesn't expect, the boor.

WESENER: Show me the letter! (*Enter* MADEMOISELLE ZIPFER-SAAT.) Oh, look who's here—Mademoiselle Zipfersaat! I'll read it downstairs in the shop.

MARIE (*curtsying mischievously all round* MADEMOISELLE ZIPFERSAAT): Mademoiselle Zipfersaat, allow me to present a baron who is mortally enamored of you. Here, Baron, this is the young lady that we talked about so much and that you took such a mortal fancy to at the play the other day.

MADEMOISELLE ZIPFERSAAT: I don't know what's got into you, Marie!

MARIE (*dropping a deep curtsy*): Now you can declare your love!

(MARIE *runs off, banging the door behind her.* MADEMOISELLE ZIPFERSAAT *is embarrassed and goes over to the window.* DESPORTES, *having cast a contemptuous glance at her, keeps a lookout for* MARIE, *who opens the door briefly every now and then. Eventually she puts her head round the door.*)

MARIE (*mockingly*): Well, are you nearly finished?

(DESPORTES *tries to stick his foot in the door,* MARIE *chases him away with a large pin; he shouts and suddenly runs off to get at* MARIE *through a door on the other side of the stage.* MADEMOISELLE ZIPFERSAAT *goes off in high dudgeon, while shouts, screams, and giggles come from the room next door.* WESENER'S MOTHER *creeps into the room, spectacles on her nose, sits down in the window nook and begins to knit, singing— or rather screeching—in a hoarse old voice.*)

WESENER'S MOTHER:

> A maiden young is like the dice
> And lies as she is tumbled,
> The little rose from Hennegau
> Goes soon to Our Lord's table.
> (*Counts the stitches.*)
> Why smile you then so gay, my child,
> A cross you soon must carry;
> The little rose from Hennegau,
> They say, is soon to marry.

Oh, child of mine, how sad am I,
While still your eyes are smiling,
For soon a thousand tears you'll cry,
That stain your cheeks beguiling.
(*In the meantime the laughing and teasing
continues in the next room. The old woman goes in
to rebuke them.*)

ACT THREE

SCENE ONE

Armentières. AARON's *house.* RAMMLER *enters with a
number of heavily cloaked men, whom he posts at
various points.*

RAMMLER (*to the last of his men*): If anyone goes in, then
cough. I'll hide under the steps so I can creep up after him.
(*Crawls into hiding under the steps.*)

AARON (*looks out of the window*): Got, vot iss zis for a plotting
going on before my very house?

(MURRAY *wrapped in a topcoat, comes down the lane, stops
below* AARON's *window and whistles quietly.*)

AARON (*calls down to him sotto voce*): Iss it you, sir? (MURRAY
gives a signal.) I vill at once open ze door. (MURRAY *goes up
the steps. Someone coughs softly.* RAMMLER *follows* MURRAY
on tiptoe without MURRAY's *looking round.* AARON *opens the
door, and* RAMMLER *slips in behind* MURRAY. *The scene
changes to* AARON's *bedroom. It is very dark.* MURRAY *and*
AARON *are whispering to each other.* RAMMLER *prowls
round them, darting back every time they make a movement.*)

MURRAY: He's in here somewhere.

AARON: Oi vai!

MURRAY: Keep quiet and he'll do you no harm; let him do what
he wants with you, even if he ties you up. I'll be back in a
minute with the town watchmen. He'll pay for it all right.
Lie down on the bed.

AARON: But vot if he take my life, eh?

MURRAY: Don't worry, I'll be back in a moment. He can't be
convicted unless he's caught in the act. The watch are

downstairs all ready, I'll just go and fetch them in. Lie down. (*Goes out.* AARON *lies down on the bed.* RAMMLER *creeps nearer to him.*)

AARON (*his teeth chattering*): Adonai! Adonai!

RAMMLER (*to himself*): I do believe it's a Jewess. (*Aloud, trying to imitate* MURRAY'*s voice.*) Oh, my darling, how cold it is outside.

AARON (*more and more faintly*): Adonai!

RAMMLER: You know me, don't you? I'm not your husband, I'm Murray. (*Takes off his boots and tunic.*) I think we shall have snow, it's so cold.

(MURRAY *rushes in with a crowd of officers carrying lanterns; they burst into loud laughter.* AARON *starts up in terror.*)

HAUDY: Have you gone crazy, Rammler? What lewdness are you up to with the Jew?

RAMMLER (*stands as if petrified. After a while he draws his sword*): I'll make mincemeat of you, the whole damned lot of you! (*Runs out in confusion. The others laugh even louder.*)

AARON: Got knows, I been half dead already! (*Stands up. The officers rush out in pursuit of* RAMMLER, AARON *follows them.*)

SCENE TWO

STOLZIUS' *house. He is sitting, a cloth around his head, at a table with a lighted lamp on it. He has a letter in his hand. His mother is standing beside him.*

MOTHER (*suddenly losing her temper*): Won't you get off to bed, you godless creature! What's the matter with you! You were far too good for that slut! What are you grieving for, why are you whining over that . . . soldier's whore!

STOLZIUS (*in a towering rage, getting up from the table*): Mother!

MOTHER: What else is she then? And you, too, hanging round such trollops!

STOLZIUS (*catches hold of both her hands*): Dear mother, don't malign her, she's innocent, that officer has turned her head!

Look how she used to write to me. It's enough to drive me out of my mind! A good-hearted girl like that!

MOTHER (*stamps her foot*): A slut like that! Go to bed, I order you! What's going to come of all this, how will it all end? I'll show you, young man, that I'm your mother!

STOLZIUS (*striking his chest with clenched fist*): My little Marie! No, she's not my Marie any more, she's not what she was! (*Jumps up.*) Leave me alone!

MOTHER (*weeping*): Where are you off to, you God-forsaken boy?

STOLZIUS: That fiend who corrupted her, I'll ... (*Falls exhausted onto his chair, holding up his hands.*) Oh, you shall pay for this, you shall pay for this! (*Coldly.*) One day is just like another: what doesn't come to pass today will come to pass tomorrow, and what comes slowly still comes surely. What does it say in the song, mother? If a little bird carried away a single grain of sand from a mountain every year, in the end it would carry off the whole mountain.

MOTHER: I believe you're wandering in your mind! (*Feels his pulse.*) Lie down, Charles, I beg you, for heaven's sake! I'll tuck you up warm, what will come of it all, God in heaven? You're all in a fever ... and all for the sake of a strumpet like that ...

STOLZIUS: At last, at last ... every day a tiny grain of sand, a year has ten, twenty, thirty, a hundred ... (MOTHER *tries to lead him away.*) Leave me alone, mother, I'm quite all right.

MOTHER: Come along, come along! (*Dragging him away.*) Fool! I shan't leave you, believe me. (*Exeunt.*)

SCENE THREE

Lille. MADEMOISELLE ZIPFERSAAT; *a* MAID *from* WESENER's *house.*

MADEMOISELLE ZIPFERSAAT: She's at home, but won't see anyone? Well, I must say! Has she turned so proud?

MAID: She says she's busy, she's reading a book.

MADEMOISELLE ZIPFERSAAT: Tell her I've some news for her that she wouldn't miss for the world.

(MARIE *enters with a book in her hand.*)

MARIE (*offhandedly*): Good morning, Mademoiselle Zipfersaat. Why didn't you sit down?

MADEMOISELLE ZIPFERSAAT: I only came to tell you that Baron Desportes has run away.

MARIE (*in great excitement*): What's that you say?

MADEMOISELLE ZIPFERSAAT: You can believe me all right; he cleared off owing my cousin over seven hundred livres, and when they went into his room they found all his things gone and a note on the table saying they needn't bother to follow him, he had taken his discharge and was off to join the Austrians.

MARIE (*runs out sobbing and calls her father*): Papa, papa!

WESENER: What's the matter?

MARIE: Come up here quickly, dear papa!

MADEMOISELLE ZIPFERSAAT: There, you see what these officers and gentlemen are like, I could have told you so all along.

WESENER (*enters*): Well, what is it? . . . Your servant, Mademoiselle Zipfersaat.

MARIE: Papa, what shall I do? That Desportes has run away!

WESENER: Now, then, who's been telling you such fairy tales?

MARIE: He's seven hundred livres in debt to young Monsieur Zipfersaat, the silk merchant, and he left a note on the table saying he'll never come back to Flanders as long as he lives.

WESENER (*very angry*): What sort of confounded evil gossip is this . . . (*Striking himself on the chest.*) I'll go surety for that seven hundred livres, you understand, Mademoiselle Zipfersaat? And for as much again, if you want. I've done business with that family for over thirty years, but it's all the fault of those jealous good-for-nothings . . .

MADEMOISELLE ZIPFERSAAT: My cousin will be delighted, Monsieur Wesener, if you take it upon yourself to save the Baron's good name.

WESENER: I'll go with you this moment. (*Looks for his hat.*) I'll stop their mouths: how dare they bring my house into disrepute! Understand?

MARIE: But papa . . . (*Impatiently.*) Oh, I wish I had never set eyes on him!

(*Exeunt* WESENER *and* MADEMOISELLE ZIPFERSAAT.)

MARIE (*throws herself into the armchair; after sitting plunged in thought for a moment she calls timidly*): Lottie! Lottie!

(*Enter* CHARLOTTE.)

CHARLOTTE: Well, what do you want? Why were you calling me?

MARIE (*goes up to her*): Lottikins! My dearest Lottikins! (*Strokes her chin.*)

CHARLOTTE: Heaven help us, what's all this about?

MARIE: You *are* my dearest, kindest Charlotte, aren't you?

CHARLOTTE: I suppose you want to borrow money from me again.

MARIE: I'll do whatever you want.

CHARLOTTE: Oh, come on! I'm not going to waste my time on you. (*Makes as if to go out.*)

MARIE (*stops her*): But listen . . . just a moment . . . can't you help me write a letter?

CHARLOTTE: I haven't time.

MARIE: Just a couple of lines. I'll let you have my beads that cost six livres.

CHARLOTTE: Who do you want to write to, then?

MARIE (*shamefacedly*): To Stolzius.

CHARLOTTE (*starts to laugh*): Is your conscience pricking you?

MARIE (*half crying*): Don't . . .

CHARLOTTE (*sits down at the table*): Well, what do you want me to write to him, then? You know I don't like writing.

MARIE: My hands are trembling so . . . Write at the top—or all in one line, if you like: "My very dear friend."

CHARLOTTE: "My very dear friend . . ."

MARIE: "In your last letter you gave me the opportunity, as was only proper, since my good name had been called in question . . ."

CHARLOTTE: "Called in question . . ."

MARIE: "Nevertheless you mustn't look too closely at everything I say, but have regard to my heart, that . . ." Wait a moment, what shall I write now?

CHARLOTTE: How should I know?

MARIE: Tell me, what's the word I want?

CHARLOTTE: How should I know what you want to write to him?

MARIE: "That my heart and . . ." (*Begins to weep and throws herself into the armchair.*)

CHARLOTTE (*looks at her and laughs*): Well, what am I to write to him?

MARIE (*sobbing*): Write whatever you like.

CHARLOTTE (*writes and then reads aloud*): "That my heart is not as fickle as you may think." Is that all right?

MARIE (*jumps up and looks over her shoulder*): Yes, that's right, that's right! (*Embracing* CHARLOTTE.) Dear old Lottie!

CHARLOTTE: Watch out, let me finish writing!

(MARIE *walks up and down once or twice; then suddenly she rushes up to* CHARLOTTE, *snatches the paper from her, and tears it into fragments.*)

CHARLOTTE (*furious*): What are you doing? You hussy! Just when I had my very best idea! You baggage!

MARIE: Baggage yourself!

CHARLOTTE (*threatens* MARIE *with the inkwell*): You . . .!

MARIE: You're just trying to upset me all the more when I'm unhappy enough as it is!

CHARLOTTE: You hussy! What did you want to tear it up for, just when I was writing so well?

MARIE (*heatedly*): Don't you swear at me!

CHARLOTTE (*half crying also*): Why did you tear it up, then?

MARIE: Do you want me to tell him lies? (*Begins to sob passionately and throws herself down, burying her face in a chair.*)

(WESENER *enters.* MARIE *looks up and rushes to him, throwing her arms round his neck.*)

MARIE (*trembling*): Papa, dear papa! What's the news? For heaven's sake, tell me!

WESENER: Don't be so foolish, he's not vanished from the face of the earth. You do carry on so!

MARIE: But if he's gone . . .

WESENER: If he's gone, he'll have to come back, that's all. I believe you've taken leave of your senses and you're trying

to drive me crazy as well! I've known his family longer than
just since yesterday; they won't want any scandal. Now then,
send up to our attorney and see if he's at home. I'll have that
credit I signed for Desportes certified, and also the copy of the
Promesse de Mariage, and I'll send all the papers to his
parents.

MARIE: Oh, Papa, dear papa! I'll run up myself this very
minute and fetch him. (*Rushes off helter-skelter.*)

WESENER: May God forgive me, but that girl could make
Louis XIV himself lose heart! But it really is too bad of
Monsieur le Baron, I'll see he gets a warm reception from
his father. Just wait! Where is she then? (*Goes after*
MARIE.)

SCENE FOUR

Armentières. Promenade by the old moat. EISENHARDT
and PIRZEL *strolling.*

EISENHARDT: Murray means to spend his furlough in Lille;
what might that signify, I wonder? He has no relatives
there, as far as I know.

PIRZEL: He's not a man of much discernment. Flighty,
flighty! But the lieutenant-colonel: there's a man for you!

EISENHARDT (*aside*): Oh dear, how can I haul him out of his
metaphysics? (*Aloud.*) In order to understand men, in my
estimation, one ought to begin with women.

(PIRZEL *shakes his head violently.*)

EISENHARDT (*aside*): He has far too much of what the others
lack! Oh, the profession of arms and its appalling celibacy:
what freaks it makes of men!

PIRZEL: With women, you say! That's like beginning with
sheep. No, what a man is . . . (Lays his forefinger against
his nose.)

EISENHARDT (*aside*): He'll philosophize me into the grave!
(*Aloud.*) I have observed that one can scarcely step outside
the city gates this time of year without seeing a soldier caress-
ing a wench.

PIRZEL: That's because people don't think.

EISENHARDT: But doesn't thinking interfere with your drill sometimes?

PIRZEL: Not a bit of it, it's quite automatic. The other fellows aren't thinking either, they've got visions of pretty girls in front of their eyes the whole time.

EISENHARDT: That must make for rather odd battles. A whole regiment with its wits bemused can hardly fail to perform prodigies of valor.

PIRZEL: All automatic!

EISENHARDT: Yes, but you march automatically as well. The Prussian bullets must sometimes have given you a rude awakening from your sweet dreams. (*They walk on.*)

SCENE FIVE

Lille. MURRAY's *quarters.* MURRAY, STOLZIUS *dressed as a soldier.*

MURRAY (*sketching, looks up*): Who's there? (*Looks hard at* STOLZIUS, *then stands up.*) Stolzius?

STOLZIUS: Yes, sir.

MURRAY: Where the dickens have you sprung from? And in that tunic? (*Turns* STOLZIUS *round.*) You've changed; you've grown so haggard and pale! You could have told me a hundred times you were Stolzius and I wouldn't have believed it.

STOLZIUS: That's the moustache, sir. I heard you needed a batman, and seeing as the Colonel knows me well he gave me his permission to come here and at least help you enlist a few recruits and act as your servant.

MURRAY: Bravo! You're a first-class fellow! And I'm glad you're in the King's service. What's the good of that humdrum cheap-jack's life anyway? And you're in a position to afford some little extras, live decently, and get on in the world. I'll see you're all right, you can depend on that. Come along, I'll see about a room for you; you shall spend the winter with me, I'll square things with the Colonel.

STOLZIUS: As long as I pay someone to do my guard duties, no one can lay a finger on me. (*Exeunt.*)

SCENE SIX

Lille. MADAME WESENER, MARIE, CHARLOTTE.

MADAME WESENER: It's a disgrace, the way you carry on with him. I can't see where the difference is, you treat him just like you treated Desportes.

MARIE: What else can I do, mama? If he's Desportes' best friend and the only one who can get us news of him.

CHARLOTTE: If he didn't give you so many presents you'd be quite different with him.

MARIE: Am I supposed to throw his presents back in his face? I have to be civil to him because he's the only one who still writes to Desportes. If I scare him off, we'll be in a fine pickle. Desportes gets hold of all the letters that papa writes to his father and stops them reaching him, you know that.

MADAME WESENER: Once and for all, you're not to go out driving with that man! I won't have it!

MARIE: Then you come too, mama! He's ordered a horse and cabriolet. Are they to be sent away again?

MADAME WESENER: What's that to me?

MARIE: Then you come, Lottie. What am I to do now? Mama, you know what I put up with for your sake.

CHARLOTTE: Cheeky into the bargain!

MARIE: You be quiet!

CHARLOTTE (*under her breath*): Army whore!

MARIE (*behaves as if she hadn't heard* CHARLOTTE, *carries on preening herself in front of the mirror*): If we offend Murray, then we have only ourselves to blame.

CHARLOTTE (*aloud, marching out of the room*): Army whore!

MARIE (*turns round from the mirror*): Look, mama! (*Clasping her hands.*)

MADAME WESENER: Who can help you? It's the way you behave.

(*Enter Murray.*)

MARIE (*puts on a cheerful expression: goes up to him with the greatest gaiety and friendliness*): Good morning, Monsieur de Murray! Did you sleep well?

MURRAY: Supremely well, mademoiselle! I saw last night's fireworks all over again in my dreams.

MARIE: It was beautiful.

MURRAY: It must have been, if it had your approval.

MARIE: Oh, I am no expert in these matters, I'm merely repeating what I heard you say. (*He kisses her hand; she drops a deep curtsy.*) We're in dreadful disarray; my mother will be ready in a moment.

MURRAY: Madame Wesener? You mean to come with us?

MADAME WESENER (*drily*): What's that? Is there no room for me?

MURRAY: Oh, yes. I shall climb up behind, and my man can run on ahead.

MARIE: Tell me, your servant has a strong resemblance to a certain person that I used to know; he wanted to marry me.

MURRAY: And you turned him down. I expect Desportes was partly to blame for that.

MARIE: He got his own back on me anyway.

MURRAY: Shall we? (*He offers his arm to* MARIE, *she curtsys and points to her mother; he gives* MADAME WESENER *his arm, and* MARIE *follows them out.*)

SCENE SEVEN

Philippeville. DESPORTES *alone in his shirtsleeves in a room with green wallpaper, writing a letter, a lighted candle in front of him.*

DESPORTES (*muttering to himself as he writes*): I'll have to keep her sweet, otherwise there will be no end to this letter writing, and sooner or later one of them will fall into my father's hands. (*Reads his letter.*) "Your esteemed father is angry with me because I have kept him waiting so long for his money; please pacify him until I have a chance to reveal everything to my father and persuade him to give his consent so that you may be mine, my darling, for ever and ever. Remember, I am greatly worried lest he should have intercepted some of your letters, for I see from your last that you must have written many that I never received. And that might well wreck all our plans. I beg you not to write to me until I have sent you a new address where I can safely receive your letters." (*Seals the letter.*) If only I could make Murray fall in love with her, so that she could forget me! I'll write and tell him he mustn't stir from my side when I have made my adorable Marie happy; he shall be her paramour! Just wait! (*Strides up and down deep in thought, then goes off.*)

SCENE EIGHT

Lille. COUNTESS DE LA ROCHE's *residence.* COUNTESS,
FOOTMAN.

COUNTESS (*looks at her watch*): Has the young gentleman not come home yet?

FOOTMAN: No, madame.

COUNTESS: Give me the key to the front door and go to bed. I shall open the door to him myself. How is young Catherine?

FOOTMAN: She had a high fever this evening.

COUNTESS: Go in to her again and see whether the governess is still awake. Tell her I'm not going to bed. I'll come and take her place at one o'clock. (*Exit* FOOTMAN.)

COUNTESS: Must a child cause his mother pain right to the grave? Were you not my son, and had I not endowed you with a heart so full of tender feeling . . . (*Loud knocking at the door.* COUNTESS *goes out and then returns with the* YOUNG COUNT.)

YOUNG COUNT: But, mother, where's the footman? These confounded people, if only it weren't so late I'd send for the watch and have them break every bone in the fellow's body!

COUNTESS: Gently, gently, my son! Supposing I were as impatient with you as you are with this blameless man?

YOUNG COUNT: It's absolutely insufferable!

COUNTESS: I sent him to bed myself. Isn't it enough that the fellow has to look after you the whole day long? Is he to lose his night's sleep, too, on account of you? I do believe you'd have me look upon our servants as beasts of burden.

YOUNG COUNT (*kisses her hand*): Dear mother!

COUNTESS: I must talk to you seriously, young man! You are beginning to darken my days with care. You know I have never attempted to curb you; I have shared in your concerns as your friend, never as your mother. Why have you begun lately to make a secret of your *affaires de cœur*, when formerly you concealed none of your youthful follies from me, since I, too, am a woman and was always able to give you the best of advice. (*Looks at him severely*.) You're in a fair way to becoming a rake, my son!

YOUNG COUNT (*weeps, kisses his mother's hand*): Dear mother, I swear that I have no secrets from you. You happened to meet me after supper with Mademoiselle Wesener; you drew conclusions from the hour and from the manner in which we were conversing . . . she's an amiable girl, nothing more.

COUNTESS: I do not seek to know more. The moment you have reason to believe you are obliged to conceal something from me . . . but remember that you will have yourself to blame afterwards for the consequences of your actions. Mademoiselle Anklam has relatives here, and I know Mademoiselle Wesener does not enjoy the best of reputations—through no fault of her own, I understand: they say the poor child was led astray.

YOUNG COUNT (*kneeling down*): Exactly, dear mother! It's her misfortune, in fact . . . if you but knew the circumstances. Yes, I must tell you everything, I feel I am involved in the girl's fate . . . And yet . . . How easily was she deceived, a carefree, open, blameless heart! It grieves me, mama, that she did not fall into worthier hands.

COUNTESS: Leave compassion to me, my son. Believe me, (*embraces him*) believe me, my heart is no more obdurate than yours. But compassion is for me less perilous. Listen to my advice, do what I say. For the sake of your peace of mind, don't go back there again, leave the town, go to Mademoiselle Anklam . . . and be assured no harm will befall Mademoiselle Wesener here. In me you are leaving her a most affectionate friend. Do you promise me you will do as I say?

YOUNG COUNT (*looks long and lovingly at her*): Yes, mama, I promise to do everything you ask. Just one word before I go. She is the victim of misfortune, poor girl, that much is certain.

COUNTESS: Don't worry. (*Patting his cheek.*) I believe you; you need not convince me of that.

YOUNG COUNT (*rises to his feet and kisses her hand*): I know you . . . (*Exeunt.*)

SCENE NINE

Lille. MADAME WESENER, MARIE.

MARIE: Let me be, mama! I mean to tease him.

MADAME WESENER: Get along with you! What? He's forgotten you, he hasn't been here for three days, and everybody says he's fallen in love with that little Madame Duval in the rue de Bruxelles.

MARIE: You wouldn't believe how obliging the Count is to me.

MADAME Wesener: Oh, come! They say he's already promised.

MARIE: Then I'll tease Murray about the Count. He's coming again this evening after dinner. If only Murray could see me and the Count some time when he's with that Madame Duval of his. (*A* FOOTMAN *enters.*)

FOOTMAN: Countess de la Roche begs to know whether you are at home.

MARIE (*in great confusion*): Oh, heavens, the Count's mother! Tell her . . . Mama, tell me, what should he say?

(MADAME WESENER *gets up to go.*)

MARIE: Say it will be a great honor . . . Mama, mama, say something!

MADAME WESENER: Can't you open your mouth? Say it will be a great honor for us, although we're in a dreadful mess here.

MARIE: No, no, wait a moment, I'll come down to the carriage myself.

(MARIE *goes downstairs with the footman. Exit* MADAME WESENER.)

SCENE TEN

COUNTESS DE LA ROCHE *and* MARIE *enter.*

MARIE: Excuse us, madame, everything's in a great muddle.

COUNTESS: My dear child, pray do not trouble yourself in the slightest on my account. (*Takes* MARIE's *hand and sits down on the sofa with her.*) Look upon me as your very best friend. (*Kissing her.*) I do assure you, I take the most sincere interest in everything that can possibly affect you.

MARIE (*wiping her eyes*): I do not know how I have deserved this exceptional favor you show me.

COUNTESS: Do not speak of favors, I beg of you. I am glad we are alone; I have a great many things to tell you that are near my heart, and a number of things to ask you as well. (MARIE *listens attentively with a joyfully expectant expression.*) I love you, my angel! I cannot but confess this love. (MARIE *kisses the* COUNTESS's *hand fervently.*) Your whole manner has something so frank and so engaging that your misfortune is doubly painful to me. Do you know, my dear new friend, that there is much talk of you in the town?

MARIE: I know all too well that there are spiteful tongues in every place.

COUNTESS: Not just spiteful tongues, virtuous tongues are talking of you as well. You are unfortunate, but you may console yourself with the thought that you have not incurred your misfortune through any vice. Your only fault was lack of acquaintance with the ways of the world: you did not acknowledge that disparity which prevails between the different classes of society; you have been reading *Pamela*, the most pernicious book that a person in your station of life can possibly read.

MARIE: I have never even heard of the book.

COUNTESS: Then you have placed too great a trust in what young gentlemen have told you.

MARIE: There is only one person I trusted too much, and it is not yet certain that he has been unfaithful to me.

COUNTESS: Good, my dear young friend! But tell me, pray, how did you come to look for a husband above your station?

Your figure, so you thought, could carry you further than other girls of your acquaintance. Oh, dear young friend, that is precisely what should have rendered you more circumspect! Good looks were never the means to found a good marriage, and no one has more cause to tremble than the possessor of a fair countenance. A thousand perils masked with blossoms, a thousand worshipers and not a single friend, a thousand pitiless seducers!

MARIE: Oh, madame, I know very well that I am homely.

COUNTESS: Enough of this false modesty! You are beautiful, heaven has inflicted the penalty of beauty upon you. You have met people above your station who made you promises. You saw no difficulty in rising to a higher level, you despised the playmates of your youth, you felt it unnecessary to acquire other amiable qualities, you shrank from hard work, you treated young men of your own class with contempt and were detested in return. Poor child! How happy you might have made some respectable citizen, had you only imbued these unblemished features, this engaging manner with a modest and charitable spirit: how you would have been cherished by your equals, emulated and admired by your betters! But you sought the envy of your peers. Poor child, what were you thinking of, and for what wretched fortune did you seek to exchange these merits? To become the wife of a man who would on your account be detested and despised by all his family! And to hazard your entire happiness, your entire honor, even your life on such an ill-starred game of chance! What were you thinking of, what were your parents thinking of? Poor misguided child, victim of vanity! (*Clasps* MARIE *to her breast.*) I would have given my life's blood to prevent this happening!

MARIE (*weeping on the* COUNTESS's *hand*): But he loved me!

COUNTESS: The love of an officer, Marie! Of a man who is hardened to every kind of debauchery and infidelity, who ceases to be a good soldier the moment he becomes a faithful lover, who swears to his king that he will not be any such thing and has himself hired on this understanding. And you thought you were the one person in the world who could keep him faithful—in spite of the wrath of his parents, in spite of family pride, in spite of his oath, in spite of his character, in spite of the whole world. That is, you sought to turn the world upside down—and now you see you have failed you think to carry out your plan with others, and do not observe that what you take for love in them is nothing but compassion with your fate, or something worse. (MARIE *falls on her knees in front of the* COUNTESS, *hides her face in the* COUNTESS's *lap, and sobs.*) Make up your mind, dearest child! Unhappy girl, there is still time, you may still escape the pit, I'll risk my life to draw you back from the brink! Abandon all your designs on my son; he is promised already, Mademoiselle Anklam has his hand and his heart. But come and live with me. Your honor has suffered a severe blow; this is the only way to restore it. Be my companion, and resolve to shun male company for a whole year. You shall help me bring up my daughter. Come, we shall go to your mother straight away and ask her permission for you to come with me.

MARIE (*raises her head pathetically from the* COUNTESS's *lap*): Madame, it is already too late.

COUNTESS (*hastily*): It is never too late to be sensible. I'll furnish you with a thousand livres for your dowry; I know your parents have debts.

MARIE (*still on her knees, almost falling over backwards, with clasped hands.*) Oh, madame, permit me to think it over . . . to put it to my mother.

COUNTESS: Very well, my dear child, do your best. You will have entertainment enough in my house. I'll have you instructed in sketching, dancing, and singing.

MARIE (*falls forward on her face*): Oh, too, too generous madame!

COUNTESS: I must leave: your mother would find me in a strange state of mind. (*Goes off quickly, looks back from the door at* MARIE, *who is still on her knees, as if in prayer.*) Farewell, child! (*Exit.*)

ACT FOUR

SCENE ONE

Lille. MURRAY, STOLZIUS.

MURRAY: Let me tell you frankly, Stolzius, if Desportes doesn't marry the girl, I'll marry her myself. I'm madly in love with her. I've done my best to turn my thoughts elsewhere, as you well know, with that Duval woman . . . and then I don't care for that business with the Count, and what with the Countess taking the girl to live with her now . . . but still, all that—is neither here nor there, I can't get the foolish notion out of my head.

STOLZIUS: Doesn't Desportes write any more, then?

MURRAY: To be sure he writes! Only the other day his father tried to force him into a marriage and locked him up for a couple of weeks on bread and water. (*Striking his head with his fist.*) And when I think how she went for a stroll in the moonlight with me not long ago and told me about her troubles, how sometimes she jumped up in the middle of the night to look for a knife when gloomy thoughts came over her.

(STOLZIUS *trembles.*)

MURRAY: I asked her if she loved me. She said she loved me more tenderly than any of her friends and relatives and pressed my hand against her breast.

(STOLZIUS *turns his face toward the wall.*)

MURRAY: And when I asked her to give me a kiss, she said, if it were in her power to make me happy, she'd do it for sure. But I would need leave from Desportes. (*Seizes hold of* STOLZIUS *roughly.*) Devil take me, man, if I don't marry her, supposing Desportes leaves her in the lurch!

STOLZIUS (*very coldly*): They say she's very well in with the Countess.

MURRAY: If only I knew a way to talk to her. Go and make inquiries!

SCENE TWO

Armentières. DESPORTES *in prison,* HAUDY *visiting him.*

DESPORTES: I'm glad I'm in jail, no one will find out I'm here.

HAUDY: I'll tell our comrades not to breathe a word.

DESPORTES: Murray mustn't find out, that's the most important thing.

HAUDY: Nor must Rammler. He sets himself up as such a great friend of yours: he says he joined the regiment a few weeks after you on purpose to allow you the seniority.

DESPORTES: The idiot!

HAUDY: Listen, we had another joke with him not long ago that will make you laugh your head off. You know that Gilbert lodges with an old hunchbacked, cross-eyed widow, just for the sake of her good-looking cousin. He gives a concert in the house once a week just to please this wench. Our Rammler gets a skinful one night; he thinks the cousin sleeps in the house so he creeps away from dinner and in his usual crafty way sneaks into the widow's bedroom, strips, and lies down in the bed. The widow, who's had a bit to drink too, lights her cousin home to where she lives just nearby. We all think Rammler has cleared off home; she goes upstairs to her room, is about to get into bed, and finds our gentleman there in a great state of confusion. He excuses himself and says he didn't know where the convenience was, she carts him downstairs without much ado, and we almost split our sides. He begged us for God's sake not to tell a soul about it. But you know what Gilbert is like, he told the girl the whole story, and she put it into the old woman's head that Rammler's in love with her. As a matter of fact, he has rented a room in her house—perhaps to make sure she keeps her mouth shut. And now you'd have the laugh of your life to see him and the old baggage together in company. She simpers and ogles him and twists up her lopsided wrinkled old mug. You could die laughing, and him with his red hawk's beak and his eyes popping out of his head—you can't even think about it without laughing yourself to death!

SCENE THREE

Lille. A garden at the residence of COUNTESS DE LA ROCHE. COUNTESS *in an avenue.*

COUNTESS: What can be the matter with the girl that she's gone down into the garden so late? I fear, I very much fear she has an assignation. She does her sketching absent-mindedly, plays the harp absent-mindedly, she's always woolgathering when her language master tells her something . . . Hark, I can hear someone . . . yes, she's up in the summerhouse, and somebody's talking to her from the road. (*Puts her ear to the hedge.*)

MURRAY'S VOICE (*offstage*): Is it fair to forget all your friends, everything you once cared for?

MARIE'S VOICE (*offstage*): Oh, dear Monsieur Murray, I'm sorry enough for it, but it must be so. I assure you, the Countess is the sweetest lady on God's earth.

MURRAY (*offstage*): But it's as if you were in a nunnery. Won't you ever come back into the world? You know that Desportes has written; he's inconsolable, he wants to know where you are and why you don't reply to him.

MARIE (*offstage*): Really? Ah, I must forget him; tell him that and say that he must forget me.

MURRAY (*offstage*): But why? Heartless girl! Is it fair to treat your friends like this?

MARIE (*offstage*): There's no other way. Oh, God, I can hear someone in the garden down there! Farewell, farewell! Cherish no false hopes . . . (*Climbs down.*)

COUNTESS: So, Marie! You have assignations!

MARIE (*gives a terrified start*): Oh, madame ... it was a relative of mine ... my cousin ... and he's only just discovered where I am ...

COUNTESS (*gravely*): I heard everything.

MARIE (*half on her knees*): Oh, God, forgive me, just this once!

COUNTESS: You're like that sapling there in the evening breeze, girl: every breath of wind sways you. What are you thinking of, do you think you can pick up the threads of your affair with Desportes here under my very eyes? Do you think you can have secret meetings with his friends? Had I known that, I would never have bothered with you.

MARIE: Pardon me, just this once!

COUNTESS: I shall never pardon you when you act against your own best interests. Begone!

(MARIE *goes off in despair.*)

COUNTESS: I cannot tell whether I am right to rob the girl of her romance, in all conscience. What charms does life retain if our imagination does not introduce them? Eating, drinking, occupations without future prospects, without pleasures of our own making, this is naught but death delayed. She feels that and only pretends to be cheerful. If only I could discover something that would couple her imagination with my prudence, that would make her heart obey me, not just her reason.

SCENE FOUR

Armentières. DESPORTES *striding rapidly up and down with a letter in his hand.*

DESPORTES: If she comes here, I'm a ruined man—disgraced, a laughingstock among my messmates. (*Sits down and writes.*) What's more, my father mustn't see her ...

SCENE FIVE

WESENER'*s house.* WESENER, COUNTESS'S FOOTMAN.

WESENER: Marie has run away from home? She'll be the death of me yet! (*Rushes off, followed by the* FOOTMAN.)

SCENE SIX

MURRAY's *quarters.* MURRAY; STOLZIUS, *pale and
disheveled.*

MURRAY: Let's go after her then, damn it! I'm to blame for
all this. Run down and fetch horses!

STOLZIUS: If only we knew where . . .

MURRAY: Armentières! Where else can she have gone?
(*Exeunt.*)

SCENE SEVEN

WESENER's *house.* MADAME WESENER *and* CHARLOTTE
in cloaks. WESENER *enters.*

WESENER: It's no good. She's nowhere to be found. (*Clasps his
hands.*) God! Who knows where she may have drowned
herself!

CHARLOTTE: But who can tell, papa . . .

WESENER: Not a sign! The Countess's messengers have come
back, and it's barely half an hour since she was missed.
There's a horseman ridden out by each of the city gates, and
she can't have vanished from the face of the earth in so
short a time.

SCENE EIGHT

Philippeville. DESPORTES' GAMEKEEPER *with a letter
from his master in his hand.*

GAMEKEEPER: Oh, ho! Here's a fine quarry heading for my
snare! She's written to the master to say she'll come
straight to him in Philippeville. (*Looks at the letter.*) On
foot . . . poor child! I'll give you refreshment!

SCENE NINE

Armentières. A concert in the house of MADAME BISCHOF.
*A number of ladies in a circle around the orchestra,
among them* MADAME BISCHOF *and her cousin*
MADEMOISELLE BISCHOF. *Various officers, among them*
HAUDY, RAMMLER, MURRAY, DESPORTES, *and* GILBERT,
standing in conversation with the ladies.

MADEMOISELLE BISCHOF (*to* RAMMLER): And you have moved
in here as well, Baron?

(RAMMLER *bows without speaking and blushes violently.*)

HAUDY: He's taken up his lodging on the second floor, right
opposite your cousin's bedchamber.

MADEMOISELLE BISCHOF: So I heard. I congratulate my
cousin.

MADAME BISCHOF (*squints and smiles in coquettish fashion*): He,
he, he! The Baron would not have moved in here if
Monsieur Gilbert had not recommended my establishment so warmly. In any case, I treat all my gentlemen in
such a way that they can have no cause to complain of
me.

MADEMOISELLE BISCHOF: That I well believe; you get on very
well together, I'm sure.

GILBERT: All the same, there's a little something between the
two of them, otherwise Rammler wouldn't have come to
stay here.

MADAME BISCHOF: Really? (*Holds her fan in front of her face.*)
He, he, he! Since when, then, Monsieur Gilbert, since
when, then?

HAUDY: Since our last *soirée musicale*, you know, madame.

RAMMLER (*tugs* HAUDY's *sleeve*): Haudy!

MADAME BISCHOF (*strikes* HAUDY *playfully with her fan*):
Naughty Major! Must you blurt out all our little secrets?

RAMMLER: Madame! I cannot think how we come to be so
familiar, I must ask you . . .

MADAME BISCHOF (*very annoyed*): Really, sir? So now you give
yourself airs, do you? Anyway, you should esteem it a great
honor that a lady of my years and my character should be so

familiar with you. Just think how he must fancy himself, the young gentleman!

ALL THE OFFICERS: Hey, Rammler!... Fie, Rammler!... It isn't right to treat the lady so!

RAMMLER: Hold your tongue, madame, or I'll break every bone in your body and toss you out of the window!

MADAME BISCHOF (*stands up, furiously*): Come here, sir! (*Seizes his arm.*) Come here, this minute, you just try to lay a finger on me!

ALL THE OFFICERS: Up to bed, Rammler! There's a challenge for you!

MADAME BISCHOF: If you get above yourself, I'll throw you out of this house, d'you know that? And it's not all that far to your commanding officer! (*Begins to weep.*) Just think, such impertinence in my own house, the impudent lout...

MADEMOISELLE BISCHOF: There now, cousin, the Baron didn't really mean it. He was only joking. Hush now!

GILBERT: Have some sense, Rammler, I beg of you. What honor is there in insulting an old woman?

RAMMLER: The whole damn lot of you can...! (*Rushes out.*)

MURRAY: Isn't that a riot, Desportes? What's the matter with you? You're not laughing.

DESPORTES: I have dreadful pains in my chest. This catarrh will be the death of me.

MURRAY: He kills me, that crackpot Rammler! Did you see how he turned black and blue in the face from sheer fury? Anybody else would have played up to the old hag.

(STOLZIUS *comes in and tugs at* MURRAY's *sleeve.*)

MURRAY: What's up?

STOLZIUS: I hope you don't mind, Lieutenant. Can you step outside for a moment?

MURRAY: What's up, then? Have you heard something?

(STOLZIUS *shakes his head.*)

MURRAY: Well, then. (*Comes downstage with* STOLZIUS.) Tell me here.

STOLZIUS: The rats got at your best embroidered shirt last night and gnawed it. When I opened the linen cupboard, a couple of them leaped out in my face.

MURRAY: What does it matter? Put down some poison.

STOLZIUS: I have to have a sealed note from you.

MURRAY (*irritably*): Why do you have to come to me just now?

STOLZIUS: I haven't time in the evening, Lieutenant: I have to be there when the kit is issued.

MURRAY: Here, take my watch; you can seal the note with my seal. (*Exit* STOLZIUS. MURRAY *returns to the company. An orchestra starts up.*)

DESPORTES (*who has withdrawn into a corner of the room*): I can see her all the time. To hell with the thought! What can I do about it if she ends up one of them? It's all her own fault. (*Comes back to the others and falls into a dreadful fit of coughing.* MURRAY *thrusts a piece of liquorice into his mouth; he gives a start.* MURRAY *laughs.*)

SCENE TEN

Lille. WESENER's *house.* MADAME WESENER, *the* COUNTESS'S FOOTMAN.

MADAME WESENER: What's that? You say the Countess is so affected that she's taken to her bed? Please convey our most humble respects to the Countess and her daughter. My husband has gone to Armentières, because they wanted to put seals on everything in the house on account of the bail, and he's heard that Baron Desportes is supposed to be there with his regiment. We are truly sorry that the Countess has taken our misfortune so much to heart.

SCENE ELEVEN

STOLZIUS *prowling backwards and forwards in front of an apothecary's shop. It is raining.*

STOLZIUS: What are you trembling for? My tongue is so feeble, I fear I shan't be able to utter a single word. He'll guess at once from my face what I mean to do . . . And must those who suffer wrong tremble, and only those who are guilty of wrongdoing be cheerful? Who knows where she's starving now under some hedge? In with you, Stolzius! If not for him, then for your own sake! And that is all you're after! (*Goes into the shop.*)

ACT FIVE

SCENE ONE

On the road to Armentières. WESENER, *resting.*

WESENER: No, I'll not take the stagecoach, if I have to lie
here the rest of my life! My poor child cost me enough even
before she went to the Countess's; she was always keen to
act the grand lady, and her brothers and sisters shall have no
occasion to reproach her for it. My business too has been at a
standstill for two years now . . . Who knows what Desportes
is doing to her, what he's doing to all of us . . . because she's
bound to be with him. We must simply put our trust in
God. (*Sits lost in thought.*)

SCENE TWO

MARIE *on another road to Armentières, resting under a tree;
she takes a piece of dry bread from her pocket.*

MARIE: I always thought a person could live on bread and water
alone. (*Gnaws at the bread.*) Oh, if only I had a single drop
of the wine I so often threw out of the window, the wine I
used to wash my hands in when the weather was hot.
(*Writhes on the ground.*) Oh, it hurts . . . well, I'm a wretched beggar . . . (*Looks at the piece of bread.*) I cannot bring
myself to eat it, God knows. Better to starve. (*Throws the
bread away and drags herself to her feet.*) I'll crawl as far
as I can, and if I drop dead, so much the better.

SCENE THREE

MURRAY's *quarters.* MURRAY *and* DESPORTES *are sitting*
half-dressed at a small table set for supper. STOLZIUS
in the background taking napkins from a cabinet.

DESPORTES: I tell you, she was a whore from the start, and
she only took up with me because I gave her presents. As a
matter of fact, I was up to the eyes in debt on her account,
you wouldn't believe it: she'd have done me out of house
and home if I'd carried on much longer. To cut a long story
short, brother, before I know where I am, I get a letter from
the wench, she's going to come to me in Philippeville. Now,
just imagine the row, if my father had clapped eyes on
her!

(STOLZIUS *switches the napkins around so as to have an excuse*
for lingering in the room.) What was I to do? I wrote to my
gamekeeper; he was to meet her and keep her under house
arrest in my quarters until I came back to Philippeville
myself and took her back secretly to the regiment. For the
moment my father clapped eyes on her she'd be done for.
Now, my gamekeeper's a sturdy, lusty fellow; time will
weigh heavily on their hands, what with being shut up there
together . . . I'll wait and see what he makes of her. (*Laughs*
mockingly.) I let him know on the quiet that I wouldn't
mind!

MURRAY: Look here, Desportes, that's not decent!

DESPORTES: What d'you mean, not decent? What do you want
me to do? Isn't she well enough provided for if my gamekeeper marries her? A wench like that . . .

MURRAY: She was in the Countess's good books. And I'm
damned if I wouldn't have married the girl myself if that
young Count hadn't queered my pitch, because he was in
her good books as well.

DESPORTES: You'd have got a fine slut round your neck, then!
(*Exit* STOLZIUS.)

MURRAY (*calls after* STOLZIUS): See that Monsieur Desportes
gets his wine soup right away! I don't know how it was the
man got to know her: I believe she wanted to make me

jealous because I'd been giving her the cold shoulder for a day or two. All that wouldn't have made any difference, but once I went to see her, it was in the hottest of the dog days, and because of the heat she had nothing on but a thin, thin shift of muslin, and you could see her lovely legs right through it. Every time she crossed the room and the shift fluttered out behind her . . . look, I'd have given my immortal soul to spend the night with her! Now, just imagine, as luck would have it, the Count has to turn up that very day—well, you know the girl's conceit. She carried on with him like mad, either to annoy me, or else because girls like that have no notion what they're about when a gentleman of the better class favors them with a friendly look. (STOLZIUS *comes in, puts a dish in front of* DESPORTES, *and stations himself, pale as death, behind* DESPORTES' *chair.*) I felt like red-hot iron and then suddenly as cold as ice. (DESPORTES *gulps down the soup.*) I lost all my appetite for her and from that moment I've never been able to feel affection for her. Mind you, when I heard she'd run away from the Countess . . .

DESPORTES (*eating*): Why are we talking about that baggage? Let me tell you, brother, you'll do me a favor if you never mention her name again. The very thought of her bores me to death! (*Pushes the plate away.*)

STOLZIUS (*behind* DESPORTES' *chair, with distorted features*): Really?

(MURRAY *and* DESPORTES *look at him in amazement.*)

DESPORTES (*clutches his chest*): I've got dreadful pains . . . Oh!!

(MURRAY, *his eyes riveted on* STOLZIUS, *says nothing.*)

DESPORTES (*flings himself into an armchair*): Oh!! (*Writhing in agony.*) Murray!

STOLZIUS (*leaps toward* DESPORTES, *seizes him by the ears, and presses his face against his own; in bloodcurdling tones*): Marie! Marie! Marie!

(MURRAY *draws his sword and is about to run* STOLZIUS *through.*)

STOLZIUS (*turns around calmly and snatches the sword from* MURRAY's *grasp*): Spare yourself the trouble, it's done already. I shall die happy now I can take him with me.

MURRAY (*leaves his sword in* STOLZIUS' *hand and rushes out*): Help! Help!

DESPORTES: I've been poisoned!

STOLZIUS: Yes, poisoned, you seducer! And I'm Stolzius, whose bride you made a whore of. She was my bride. If you can't live without ruining women, why must you turn to those who can't resist, who believe every word you say? You are avenged, my Marie! God cannót condemn me! (*Sinks to the floor.*)

DESPORTES: Help! (*Writhes on the floor and dies also.*)

SCENE FOUR

WESENER *walking by the River Lys, lost in thought.*
Twilight. A female figure wrapped in a cloak plucks at
his sleeve.

WESENER: Leave me alone—I am not interested in such things.

WOMAN (*in a barely audible whisper*): For God's sake, sir, whatever you can spare.

WESENER: To the workhouse with you! There are wanton strumpets enough and to spare in these parts; if a man were to give to them all, he'd have his hands full and his pockets empty.

WOMAN: Sir, I've gone three days without a bite of bread; be kind and take me to an inn where I can have a sip of wine.

WESENER: You wanton creature! Aren't you ashamed to make such a proposal to a respectable man? Begone! Run after your soldiers! (*Woman goes away without replying.*)

WESENER: Somehow she sighed so deeply! How heavy my heart is! (*Takes out his purse.*) Who knows where my own daughter is begging alms at this moment? (*Runs after the woman and offers her a coin with a trembling hand.*) Here's a franc for you . . . but mend your ways!

WOMAN (*begins to weep*): Oh, God! (*Takes the money and collapses, almost fainting.*) What good is that to me?

WESENER (*turns away, wiping tears from his eyes. He addresses her in great agitation*): Where are you from?

WOMAN: That I may not say. But I am the daughter of a respectable man.

WESENER: Did your father sell fancy goods?

(*Woman remains silent.*)

WESENER: Your father was a respectable man? Stand up. I'll take you home with me. (*Tries to help her to her feet.*) Does your father live in Lille, by any chance? (*At these last words the woman throws her arms round* WESENER's *neck.*)

WESENER (*cries out*): Oh, my daughter!

MARIE: Father!

(*Both collapse on the ground; a crowd of people gathers, and they are carried off.*)

SCENE FIVE

The COLONEL's *quarters.* COUNT VON SPANNHEIM (*the* COLONEL), COUNTESS DE LA ROCHE.

COUNTESS: Have you seen the unhappy pair? I haven't the heart. The very sight of them would kill me.

COLONEL: It made me ten years older. And to think that such a thing should happen in my corps! But, madame, what can we do? It is the fate that heaven ordains for certain mortals. I'll pay all the man's debts and another thousand livres to compensate him. Then I'll see what can be done through an appeal to the villain's father on behalf of the family he has ruined and made destitute.

COUNTESS: Worthy man! Accept my warmest gratitude in these tears. She was the finest, the most lovable creature! What high hopes I had begun to cherish for her! (*She weeps.*)

COLONEL: These tears do you honor. They soften my heart as well. And why should I not weep, a man who is obliged to fight and to die for his fatherland, to see a citizen of that fatherland and his entire family plunged into irrevocable ruin by one of my subordinates.

COUNTESS: These are the consequences of celibacy among our soldiers.

COLONEL (*shrugs his shoulders*): How can it be helped? Even Homer said, I believe, that a good husband is a poor soldier, and experience confirms it. A particular idea has often occurred to me when I read the story of Andromeda. I look upon soldiers as the monster to whom from time to time an unhappy female must be sacrificed, in order that all other wives and daughters may be spared.

COUNTESS: What do you mean?

COLONEL: If only the king would found an establishment of soldiers' paramours; it's true they would have to consent to give up the exalted notions that women have of perpetual union.

COUNTESS: I much doubt whether any woman of honor could consent to that.

COLONEL: They would have to be Amazons. In this matter, it seems to me, one noble sentiment balances the other: the delicacy of womanly honor and the idea of martyrdom for the nation.

COUNTESS: How little you men know of the heart and the aspirations of women!

COLONEL: It is true the king would have to do everything in his power to render this class of society brilliant and reputable. On the other hand, he would save recruiting expenses, and the children would belong to him. Oh, I only wish someone could be found to promote this idea at court: I would soon make sources of support known to him. Those who defend the nation would in this case be its fortune; the outer security of the nation would not cancel out its inner well-being, and in a society hitherto thrown into turmoil by us the peace and prosperity of all and universal bliss would be joined in one embrace.

(*Curtain.*)

NOTES TO *THE TUTOR*

Act 1, scene 1

p. 3. *Händel's teagarden*: "Händels Kuchengarten" was well known in Leipzig. Goethe, who was a student in Leipzig, immortalized the confectioner Händel in mock-heroic verses scribbled on a wall of the establishment and reproduced in book 7 of his autobiography *Poetry and Truth (Dichtung und Wahrheit)*.

Richter's coffeehouse: situated in the "Brühl" in Leipzig. Richter also ran a coffeegarden outside the Grimma gate of the city.

Act 1, scene 2

p. 4. *the dead straight line that your wife has chalked along your beak*: refers to the belief that a hen would be hypnotized by a line drawn down its beak and prolonged on the ground in front of it.

Act 1, scene 3

p. 6. *Pintinello . . . Beluzzi*: no dancer called Pintinello is known from this period, but Carlo Beluzzi was a famous virtuoso summoned to Saint Petersburg by Catherine the Great in 1762.

Koch's theater: Heinrich Gottfried Koch (1703–75) was the manager of a dramatic company in Leipzig.

Act 1, scene 4

p. 8. *malum hydropisiacum*: dropsy. It was believed that this disease was brought on by luxurious living.

Cornelio: the Major means Cornelius Nepos (ca. 99–24 B.C.), a Roman historian. His chief work, *De viris illustribus* (*Of famous men*), was a popular school-text, both because of its subject matter and its relatively simple style.

p. 10. *Absalom*: a reference to David's leniency toward his rebellious son, 2 Samuel 18:5.

Act 1, scene 5

p. 11. *Gellert*: Christian Fürchtegott Gellert (1729–69) was one of the most popular and influential writers of the Enlightenment, called by Frederick the Great "le plus raisonnable de tous les savants allemands." Gustchen is referring to the poem *The Suicide* (*Der Selbstmord*), of which the last lines read:

> Kurz, er besieht die Spitz' und Schneide—
> Und steckt ihn langsam wieder ein.

Count Paris: Romeo's rival in *Romeo and Juliet*.

Act 2, scene 1

p. 17. *Laban*: Jacob served Laban for seven years to gain the hand of his daughter Rachel, but was beguiled into taking Leah to wife. He was obliged to serve a further seven years for Rachel. Cf. Genesis 29.

p. 18. *Hugo Grotius*: celebrated Dutch jurist and political theorist (1583–1645).

Act 2, scene 3

p. 25. *Döbblin's company*: Karl Theophilus Döbblin or Döbbelin (1727–95) was one of the celebrated actor-managers of the eighteenth century. He was in Königsberg during the seasons 1768/69 and 1769/70 while Lenz was a student there. He moved from Leipzig to Halle in 1771.

Act 2, scene 5

p. 29. *Abelard*: Pierre Abélard (1079–1142) was domestic tutor in the house of Canon Fulbert of Notre Dame in Paris when he fell in love with Fulbert's niece Héloïse, who was his pupil.

La nouvelle Héloise: famous novel by Jean Jacques Rousseau, published in 1761.

Act 2, scene 6

p. 30. *the picture of Heautontimorumenos in my big Dacier*: Heautontimorumenos is the title of a comedy by the Roman dramatist Terence: the word means "self-tormentor." Madame Anne Dacier (1650–1703) translated Terence into French; a number of editions have woodcut illustrations.

p. 31. *poor Lazarus*: presumably the wretched beggar in the parable of Lazarus and Dives (Luke 16:19–31) rather than Lazarus of Bethany who was raised from the dead by Christ (John 11:1–44).

Act 3, scene 2

p. 37. *Mandel*: i.e. "almond." *Mandelblüte* = "almond blossom."

    unus ex his: "one of those."

Act 3, scene 3

p. 40. *the high priest Eli*: cf. 1 Samuel 2:12 ff. and 4:18. Eli "honoured his sons above God," and when they were slain in battle "he fell from off the seat backward by the side of the gate, and his neck brake, and he died: for he was an old man, and heavy."

    Damon and Pythias: a legendary friendship in which each friend sought to sacrifice himself for the other. The source of the story is classical; Schiller made it the theme of his famous ballad *The Pledge* (*Die Bürgschaft*).

Act 3, scene 4

p. 42. *ariston men to hudor*: Pindar, *Olympic Odes*, I, 1: "But the best is water."

p. 44. *Corderius' Colloquia*: the French scholar Corderius Maturinus, i.e. Mathurin Cordier (1478–1564), teacher of

Calvin, published an elementary Latin textbook, *Collo-quiorum scholasticorum libri quatuor, ad pueros in latino sermone exercendos*.

Gürtler's Lexicon: four-language dictionary of Nicolaus Gürtler (1654–1711), *Lexicon latino-germanico-graeco-gallicum*.

Act 4, scene 1

p. 45. *Professor M——r*: In his edition of the play (Munich: Wilhelm Fink Verlag, 1967) Richard Daunicht conjectures that the professor in question could be Georg Friedrich Meier (1718–77), who was professor of aesthetics and philosophy in Halle.

p. 47. *the three lilies*: mark branded on convicted prostitutes.

Act 4, scene 3

p. 50. *in jure gentium*: "in international law."

in fine videbitur cuius toni: a musical maxim—"We can tell the key by the finale."

in amore omnia insunt vitia: "love contains all vices." A quotation from Terence, *The Eunuch*, act 1, verse 59.

Act 4, scene 6

p. 54. *Ochakov*: port in the Ukraine, east of Odessa. The Russians suffered a reverse there in 1771.

Prince Czartorinsky: Adam Kasimir (1734–1823), a candidate for the Polish throne after the death of August III of Saxony in 1763.

p. 56. *Elector*: the rulers of Saxony were Electors (*Kurfürsten*), i.e. members of the electoral college which chose the Holy Roman Emperor.

Act 5, scene 1

p. 58. *Hagar*: cf. Genesis 21:14. "Abraham . . . gave her the child and sent her away: and she departed and wandered in the wilderness of Beer-sheba."

Act 5, scene 3

p. 61. *frigidus per ossa*: "chilled to the bone."

Origen: Church Father (ca. 184–252) said to have emasculated himself to avoid temptation.

Evoë: exultant cry of the devotees of Bacchus.

p. 62. *Zoar*: the "little city" to which Lot first fled (Genesis 19:22) but later left to go up into the hills; it therefore signifies an intermediate stage on the flight from evil.

Essenes: Jewish sect in the time of Christ. Wenzeslaus quotes the authentic source of his information—the Jewish historian Josephus Flavius (ca. A.D. 37–100).

in amore etc.: see notes to p. 50.

lauro tempora cingam et sublimi fronte sidera pulsabit: constructed and adapted from two Odes of Horace (III, 30 and I, 1). "I shall encircle his brow with laurel and he shall touch the lofty stars with his head."

Act 5, scene 9

p. 69. *skandalon edidous, hetaire* "you have given offense, friend!"

the cultivation of flax and hemp: R. Daunicht points out that the metaphor figures in Luther's *Table Talk* (*Tischreden*).

p. 70. *tiles on the roof*: refers to a well-known passage in which Luther described his entry into Worms, where he was to face charges of heresy: "Had I known that as many devils were aiming at me as there were tiles on the roofs, I would still have ridden in."

p. 71. *Areopagus*: the Hill of Ares, near the Acropolis in Athens. It was here that the supreme court of Athens met. The court acquitted the famous hetaira Phryne when her counsel dazzled the judges by unveiling her charms.

fleshpots of Egypt: cf. Exodus 16:3.

Act 5, scene 10

p. 73. *Proh deum atque hominum fidem*: "By the truth of Gods and men!" A phrase used by Cicero.

wolf in sheep's clothing: cf. Matthew 7:15.

For it must needs be, etc.: Matthew 18:7.

O tempora, o mores: "Oh, times, oh, manners!" A common phrase in Cicero.

Valerius Maximus: author of a compendium, "Notable Deeds and Sayings" (*Factorum et dictorum memorabilium libri ix*).

de pudicitia: "On Modesty."

ut etiam oscula ad maritum sincera perferret: "that she might bring even her kisses chaste to her husband."

Etiam oscula, non solum virginitatem, etiam oscula: "Even her kisses, not just her virginity, even her kisses."

p. 74. *hireling*: cf. John 10:12. "But he that is an hireling and not the shepherd, whose own the sheep are not, seeth the wolf coming, and leaveth the sheep and fleeth.

Connubium sine prole est quasi dies sine sole: "Wedlock without children is like a day without sun."

Be fruitful and multiply: Genesis 1:22.

p. 75. *It is better to marry than to burn*: 1 Corinthians 7:9.

homuncio: "little man."

Act 5, scene 11

p. 75. *I am not fit to be called your son*: cf. the parable of the prodigal son, Luke 15.

Act 5, scene 12

p. 79. *not only the righteous*: cf. Luke 15:7.

NOTES TO *THE SOLDIERS*

Cast

In the German text one of the officers is called "Mary"; as this is liable to be confusing for the English reader the name has been altered to "Murray." When Lenz discovered that Sophie von La Roche (see Introduction, p. xx) had a son, who was in fact being tutored in Wieland's house, he tried to have the name of the Countess changed to "von Rochau," but the type had already been set (letter to Herder, March 1776). In the manuscript of the play Marie is called "Mariane": this was changed by Lenz for the printed text.

Act 1, scene 3

p. 87. *La chercheuse d'esprit*: "The Seeker after Wit"—a comic opera with text by C. S. Favart (1710–92), first performed in 1741.

Le déserteur: a very popular drama by Sebastien Mercier (1740–1814), first performed in 1770. Mercier's *Essai sur l'art dramatique*, which attacked the tradition of French Classical drama and advocated a mixture of tragedy and comedy, may well have had some influence on Lenz.

Act 1, scene 4

p. 88. *Godeau*: evidently a French actor-manager, but there seems to be no record of any real person of that name.

p. 90. *Oglei-Oglu*: Britta Titel and Hellmut Haug in their edition of the play (Goverts Verlag, 1967) suggest that the Mongol ruler Oktai, successor to Ghengis Khan, may be meant. *Oglu* is the Turkish word for "son."

Act 2, scene 2

p. 100. *Rhine air*: an interesting slip which points to the real setting of the play's action—Strasbourg (see Introduction, p. xx).

Act 2, scene 3

p. 103. *Hennegau*: French "Hainaut," the greater part of which is now a province of Belgium.

Act 3, scene 1

p. 106. *Adonai*: Hebrew invocation of the Almighty.

Act 3, scene 10

p. 118. *Pamela*: the heroine of Samuel Richardson's novel, *Pamela or Virtue Rewarded* (1741) resists the attempts of a young nobleman to seduce her until his passion turns to true love and he marries her.

Act 5, scene 3

p. 131. *. . . once I went to see her*: the scene described by Murray is reminiscent of an episode from the diary in which Lenz recorded the affair of Cleophe Fibich (see Introduction p. xx): "I found her in the most seductive of nightgowns, her long brown tresses playing round her shoulders . . ."

Act 5, scene 5

p. 133. In the original version of the final scene the Countess is made jointly responsible with the Colonel for the suggestion of tolerated concubines for soldiers; it is she who speaks the words ,"Oh, I only wish someone could be found to promote this idea at court: I would soon make sources of support known to him." Herder advised the dramatist that this immodest attitude on the part of a high-born lady would cause offense, and at his suggestion Lenz moderated the Colonel's speeches and made the reaction of the Countess much more reserved.